BASIC CONSTRUCTION MANAGEMENT

THIRD EDITION

The Superintendent's Job

Leon Rogers

Home Builder Press®
National Association of Home Builders
1201 15th Street, NW
Washington, DC 20005-2800

Basic Construction Management: The Superintendent's Job
ISBN 0-86718-406-X

© 1995 by Home Builder Press®
of the National Association of Home Builders
of the United States of America

Cover photo: © Paul D. Ramirez, Black Hawk Construction Photography

Printed in the United States of America on recycled paper

Library of Congress Cataloging-in-Publication Data

Rogers, Leon
    Basic construction management, the superintendent's job / Leon Rogers. — 3rd ed.
        p.   cm.
    Rev. ed. of: Basic construction management, the superintendent's job / Jerry Householder. 2nd ed. c1990.
    ISBN 0-86718-406-X (pbk. : alk. paper)
    1. Building—Superintendence. I. Householder, Jerry. Basic construction management, the superintendent's job. II. Title.
TH438.R612 1995
690′.837′068—dc20   95-12274
                                 CIP

For further information, please contact:

Home Builder Press®
National Association of Home Builders
1201 15th Street, NW
Washington, DC 20005-2800
(800) 223-2665

4/95 HBP/McNaugton & Gunn 3,500

recycled paper

Contents

About the Author

Leon Rogers lives in Provo, Utah, and is a leading consultant to builders on business and production management. Rogers is a former president of Wayne Homes Newark, Inc. Before coming to Wayne Homes, Rogers was a professor of Construction Management at Brigham Young University and president of Westek Construction and Consulting, a small residential construction and consulting firm.

One of the NAHB's most popular speakers, Rogers has participated in more than 200 national seminars on such topics as project management, estimating, scheduling, and financial management. He has been an active member of the NAHB Business Management and other committees for more than 15 years.

Rogers obtained a Ph.D. in Urban Planning and Construction Management at Texas A&M University and completed a master's degree in Construction Management at Colorado State University. He has worked with local Home Builders Associations and individual companies to help improve management.

Acknowledgments

The author wishes to extend special thanks to Jerry Householder, co-author of the second edition of *Basic Construction Management*. Householder currently serves as chairman of the Construction Department of Louisiana State University in Baton Rouge. He has written a number of business management books for the building industry, including *Estimating for Home Builders*, *Scheduling for Builders*, and, most recently, *Cost Control for Builders, Remodelers, and Developers*.

Thanks also to Lee Evans, The Lee Evans Group, to Wayne Homes, and to Stephen Covey for allowing excerpts and adaptations of their materials to appear in this book.

Finally, thanks to Carl Banks, of Witt-Banks Homes; Joseph Donoghy, of MLH Development; James Erwin, of Country Estate Builders, Inc.; Randy Erwin, of Heartland Homes; Mike Johnson, of Housing Software; Dean A. Kresge, of Sugar Hollow Homes; Mark Lords, of The Snyder Group, Inc.; John Tune, of John Tune Homes, Inc.; Bob Whitten, of Wayne Homes, Inc.; Allan Freedman, NAHB Builder Business Services; Dawn Harris, NAHB Personnel Department; and Regina Solomon, NAHB Labor, Safety, and Health Services for their thoughtful review of the manuscript.

This book was produced under the general direction of Kent Colton, NAHB Executive Vice President/CEO in association with NAHB staff members James Delizia, Staff Vice President, Member and Association Relations; Adrienne Ash, Assistant Staff Vice President, Publishing and Information Services; Rosanne O'Connor, Director of Publications; Sharon Lamberton, Assistant Director of Publications; John Tuttle, Publications Editor and Project Manager; David Rhodes, Art Director; and Carolyn Poindexter, Editorial Assistant.

Preface

When the first edition of *Basic Construction Management: The Superintendent's Job* was written in 1981, the world of construction was a very different place from what it is today. The manuscript was typed five different times on a state-of-the-art IBM Selectric typewriter, which cost more than a modern personal computer. Personal computers were virtually unheard of, cellular phones and fax machines had not been invented, and construction scheduling was just in its infancy. Total Quality Management was a phenomenon in Japan, but many U.S. builders and superintendents still practiced construction management largely "by the seats of their pants." Builders were just beginning to apply business management principles to residential construction projects.

Much has happened in the past 14 years. Most residential builders have computerized their operations to some extent. Home buyers have become much more sophisticated and demand more amenities, more value, better service, and higher quality than in the past. Management of construction projects has become much more complex. Cost control and analysis of cost overruns and variances are now standard practices. Computerized scheduling is becoming widely accepted. Total Quality Management has become a familiar term to many in the industry. Thanks to NAHB's educational efforts, educators in college construction management programs, industry consultants, and builders sharing ideas with each other, today's builders are better educated and better prepared than ever before. But the competition is a lot tougher. Those who have survived in this industry have done so through better management and the successful application of some very basic principles.

Superintendents today face many more demands than their predecessors. Typically, builders now offer more customization of standard designs. More innovative and complex designs result in more complex construction. Materials, methods, and costs continually change. Many superintendents now use computers daily to obtain up-to-date information on cost control, scheduling, and overall project management. It seems as if the industry expects superintendents to be supermen and superwomen.

This edition of *Basic Construction Management: The Superintendent's Job* will address these issues and update you on the latest developments in management of home building operations.

Chapter 1

The Superintendent's Job

Introduction

The superintendent's job is arguably the most critical position in any residential construction company. Whether your company builds two custom homes a year or a thousand production homes, your primary business is the construction of homes, and as the superintendent you have more control over the building operations than anyone else. In the field, there is little room for error. As one CEO said, "It doesn't matter how many homes we sell; if we can't build them under control, the rest doesn't matter." The success of the organization depends largely on your ability to manage your projects. This book has been written specifically for you, the residential construction superintendent responsible for seeing that all field work is performed properly according to plan.

Your specific responsibilities within the company may vary. In a large company, the superintendent usually reports to a project manager, who then reports on up the management line until the owner or chief executive is involved. In smaller construction companies, the superintendent, project manager, and owner are often the same person. Whether you are the company owner or several management layers away from the executive office, your number one goal as a superintendent remains the same:

Maximize profits in the long term while maintaining a standard of excellence within the homes you produce.

The profit of a construction company is the difference between the sales price and the cost of each house. Superintendents ordinarily have only limited control over the ultimate sales price of the homes they build. Through quality work-

manship and orderly jobsites, however, you exercise your greatest influence over company profits by controlling cost. Through attention to detail and good management of subcontractors, in-house labor, and materials, you can influence the final cost of any project significantly. While your influence on project cost is relatively easy to understand, your impact on the company's continuing profits in the long term may be less clear.

For example, the general philosophy of most businesses is to make the greatest possible profit for the period of time in which the company is in business. If a builder plans to build only one house and then immediately go out of business, then a short-sighted, "quick-buck" approach might yield the highest profit. Fortunately, most construction companies plan to stay in business for a long time. As a superintendent, your key to success is motivating your workers and subcontractors to bring in every project:

- on time
- within budget
- according to established quality standards

Just about every decision you make as a superintendent should be made in keeping with these three basic responsibilities. Of course, some aspects of your job may be aimed at achieving goals that don't fall directly under one of these categories. For example, you may need to oversee maintaining a safe work environment. By and large, however, your energies should always be geared toward bringing in a quality job, on time and within budget.

While this manual provides many techniques and examples with specific applications, it is not intended to teach a particular system or point of view. The purpose of this book is to teach you correct principles and concepts and provide specific examples to help you develop a system of construction supervision that will result in improved performance and maximum profits for *your* building company.

The Superintendent's Role

A superintendent's responsibilities vary greatly with the size of the company and the leadership strategy of its owners. In a large construction company, your responsibilities as a superintendent might be limited to a single jobsite, or even to a single segment of the job, such as framing or concrete work. In the majority of residential construction companies, however, your role will be much more complicated, involving the entire production phase of several homes at the same time. Therefore, you must have knowledge of every aspect of construction and be familiar with the work of every trade.

In construction management seminars across the country, builders often ask, "How many jobs should a superintendent be responsible for at one time?" The answer to this question depends on a number of factors. How many homes a year do you build? How similar are the homes? Superintendents who build from a defined set of standard plans and handle little, if any, customization should be able to manage many more homes at one time than those who build custom homes. How much owner involvement is allowed? Building on the owner's lot and according to his or her plans is entirely different from building speculative homes in a confined subdivision with no changes. Other factors determining a superintendent's role include the size and complexity of the homes, the level of subcontractor involvement versus in-house labor, the architect's involvement in construction, the proximity of jobsites to each other, and a host of other variables.

Some generalizations may be helpful, but remember that each situation is unique. If you build small- to moderate-sized homes in a particular subdivision according to standard plans, you may be able to manage 20 to 30 homes at a time. If you build one home at a time on scattered sites, you may be able to handle 10 to 12 at

a time. If you build large, totally custom homes, you may be able to manage only one to two homes at a time.

Lee Evans, considered by many to be the most widely recognized consultant in the residential construction industry, suggests another way to look at the question. According to Evans, the cost of supervision (which includes the salaries and payroll burden of the superintendent and direct assistants) should be about $1\frac{1}{2}$ percent of sales. If your sales-to-supervision ratio is less than 1 percent, the superintendent may be overworked. If it is greater than 2 percent of sales, the superintendent may be underused.

The Superintendent's Authority

The amount of authority you have as a superintendent depends upon several factors, including the size and structure of your company, the scope of the job, and your level of experience. It is essential that you understand fully the extent of your role and authority within your particular organization.

Most building companies define a superintendent's duties and authority formally by means of a job description. Job descriptions specifically define the extent of the authority of each position within the company and the interaction between the various positions in the company.

Smaller or newly formed companies may be less rigid or well defined in their organization. Such companies generally offer a superintendent greater freedom. Most builders simply want the job done right and expect the superintendent to take over and supervise the entire construction process. Whether the company is small or large, most builders are looking for self-motivated, take-charge supervisors who project this image to others. One of the keys to success is defining the role of each of the participants in the construction process.

The Superintendent as the Company's Agent

A superintendent is a construction company's agent and field representative, and unless specifically limited otherwise, all negotiations, agreements, and contracts the superintendent enters into become legal and binding. Therefore, you have a moral and legal obligation to represent a building company's position responsibly and properly. While you may not agree with all decisions made, it is your duty to put the company first and see that all established goals and objectives are achieved. Superintendents must not allow their personal interests to come between the interests of the company and other individuals such as subcontractors or clients.

As a superintendent, you direct—and often hire and fire—most construction employees and subcontractors and usually have more direct contact with people, both inside and outside the organization, than anyone else in a building company. In addition, you may often schedule subcontractors, order materials, inspect to ensure quality work, and even deal directly with customers. Therefore, you can substantially improve a company's image and reputation by being an effective superintendent.

The Superintendent's Duties

As mentioned earlier, superintendents have responsibilities in nearly every facet of the construction business. They interact with just about everyone within the company. Every company should use job descriptions to establish the duties and responsibilities of the superintendent and the lines of authority. A job description should define and document your primary responsibilities and establish a basis for performance evaluation. Job descriptions should also be specific about the relative amount of time and attention that should be devoted to each duty. Being aware of how your time is spent is an important management practice. One of the easiest ways to do this is to monitor the amount of time you spend on each task over a period of time and then make adjustments as necessary in order to improve your effectiveness as a manager. For example, if you spend too much time stamping out fires, it is a good indication that you need to spend more time planning in order to avoid future crises. A very detailed list of job responsibilities is shown in Figure 1.1. Your job description may not include all the items on this list, which is given primarily to bring to your at-

tention the extent of the responsibilities and duties of a typical superintendent.

The Superintendent as Leader

As a key member of a builder's management team, you must also add leadership to your list of superintendent responsibilities. Leadership is the ability to work with and get things done through others while winning their respect, confidence, loyalty, and cooperation. Many people still believe that leaders are "born," not made. In reality, leadership is an attribute that can be acquired and developed by anyone with the necessary motivation.

Leadership Basics

One of the keys to being a successful superintendent is understanding your role as a manager and as a leader. In his best-seller, *Principle-Centered Leadership*, Stephen Covey stresses that the distinction between management and leadership is a crucial one.* According to Covey, most people in business spend too much time managing and not nearly enough time leading. We are far less effective when we try to manage people. According to Covey, we should manage things and lead people. You manage all of the other resources at your disposal—budgets, equipment, materials, and other items. However, the human resource, your most important resource, cannot be managed; people must be led. This includes in-house construction workers, subcontractors, suppliers, and others. The old "bull-of-the-woods" superintendent is a thing of the past. You can't force people to perform. Intimidation gets you nowhere. When traditional superintendents try to force their will upon today's workers and independent subcontractors, many of them will rebel and refuse to work, or worse, they will subvert the efforts of the superintendent. Therefore, as an effective leader, you must set an example of cooperation and goodwill, coupled with discipline, to get the maximum cooperation from your subordinates. The old adage "firm but fair" still works with most people. It is much easier to listen, learn, and co-

Figure 1.1 A Superintendent's Duties

To build the project according to the company's goals for quality, a superintendent must:
- understand basic techniques and principles of each phase of construction
- supplement on-the-job experience with training (attendance at seminars and training sessions, etc.), and reading of current industry literature
- read and interpret plans and specifications
- use subcontractors whose work is known
- communicate the required standards to workers
- establish and implement procedures for inspecting worker output
- inspect materials as they are delivered
- report results of inspections to the office in a formal manner

To build the project within the budget, a superintendent must:
- be familiar with all aspects of the project budget
- use subcontractors who are financially sound
- search for subcontractors who are less expensive and deliver good quality
- suggest alternative methods or materials that are less expensive and meet the required quality standards
- check quantity of all materials against invoices
- implement procedures to minimize theft of materials, such as making materials difficult to steal by installing them as soon as possible after delivery and arranging for someone to guard at-risk projects during vulnerable periods
- keep accurate records, and report all expenditures that are not otherwise accounted for in some other manner
- establish and implement procedures for the care and maintenance of all equipment
- follow through on all established procedures for implementing change orders
- follow all established procedures related to material purchases

To build the project on schedule, a superintendent must:
- understand scheduling methods, including critical path method
- be in agreement with—or change—projected completion date
- ensure that subcontractors and suppliers are given sufficient notice
- coordinate material deliveries
- coordinate the work of all subcontractors and hired personnel
- update progress of each project on schedule diagrams (if applicable) on a daily basis
- implement recovery procedures when schedules slip

In addition to quality, budget, or scheduling duties, a superintendent must:
- establish and enforce safety rules and regulations
- work with buyers by coordinating changes according to established procedures, keeping them up to date on scheduling projections, and emphasizing quality of materials and workmanship

operate than it is to shout, be obstinate, and point fingers.

In order to obtain the best from your people, including subcontractors, you should allow them a considerable amount of discussion and input in the decision-making process. Of course, responsibility for any final decision rests with you, the superintendent, the leader. However, enlisting the cooperation of and understanding the points of those who will actually perform the work can be valuable.

With more and more building companies subcontracting almost all of their work, superintendents work directly with several different, completely independent businesspersons. The more independent these subcontractors are, the more cooperation and coordination are required. If you have a subcontractor who works regularly or exclusively for you, you still have a tremendous amount of direct control. On the other hand, if you are a small-volume builder who uses subs only on occasion, or if you award each subcontract independently based on the lowest bid, you will have a continual training and coordination problem. Developing relations with key subs in each trade and using them exclusively is a wise practice. It is critical that both the superintendent and subcontractor be clear about what each expects of the other in the working relationship. Dialogue and documentation are important in matching expectations.

Leadership Styles

Different leadership styles are characterized by the particular emphasis each places on the decision-making process. At one extreme is company-centered leadership, in which the desires and needs of the company come first. At the other extreme is the subordinate-centered leadership style, which puts the needs of employees first. The most effective leaders maintain a balance between the needs of the building company and those of the individual worker. Maintaining this balance often requires a dynamic, forceful, and flexible individual. You may find that it helps to vary your leadership style to handle each particular situation best. This process will often result in the establishment of leadership precedents—choosing an approach to accom-

plish the objectives involved in one situation and using that style for similar situations. Specific leadership styles often used in the construction industry are discussed below.

Autocratic. In this traditional style of leadership, also referred to as dictatorial leadership, superintendents keep all authority themselves and delegate little, if any, to subordinates. The key phrase is "total control." The superintendent gives complete direction and makes all decisions; discussion and suggestions are at best tolerated but not encouraged. To employ this leadership style successfully, you must become a forceful leader of people and have a high degree of proficiency in each of the crafts and skills you supervise. This leadership style is most appropriate when:

- an emergency arises and there is no time for discussion
- an extremely tight schedule must be met
- an employee directly challenges your authority as a superintendent
- an employee is stubborn or difficult to work with
- a new employee is being trained

Bureaucratic. This leadership style relies heavily on established rules, regulations, policies, and procedures to govern the organization. The leader simply enforces the various regulations. The bureaucratic approach works best when:

- activities must be performed according to a strict plan
- highly technical equipment must be installed
- specific procedures (internal or external) must be followed
- critical issues of safety are involved
- new employees are being trained
- new policies must be implemented

Democratic. The democratic or team approach to leadership allows subordinates to participate in company goal setting. Many employees today are motivated and competent enough to work well under democratic leadership. This style works best when:

- workers are well educated, experienced, and motivated

What's In a Name?

The traditional title for managers of the construction process has been "Superintendent." In the past few years, as the responsibilities of the superintendent have increased, many builders have considered a change in this title. Some builders use the title "Construction Manager" while others use the terms "Project Manager," "Construction Supervisor," or even "Builder." Many believe that the term *Superintendent* simply does not convey to the manager or to the clients the full responsibilities of a complete manager of the construction process. The title must reflect the complexity and requirements of the position. In addition, the title projects an image to customers, subcontractors, suppliers, inspectors, and others. Builders should consider what they really want to project to those who interact with the managers in their company.

A few companies use the title "Builder" for their superintendents. They want the customers to feel that the person in charge of their home is a builder who has full responsibility and authority. They want to develop a bond or a personal relationship between the builder (superintendent) and the client; a relationship where the customer is proud to say, "This is my builder." It seems to work very well for some building companies.

Another useful title is "Construction Manager." This title conveys the fullness of the responsibility that the manager of construction has. It also conveys to the customer, subcontractors, and others outside the organization that this is the person who is in charge. The Construction Manager in turn takes additional pride in his or her position and level of responsibility.

- schedules include time for subordinates to participate in decision making
- problems require long-term solutions
- grievances need to be aired and tensions relieved

A superintendent may use a democratic leadership approach when, for example, a company is seeking to improve the compensation or bonus system for employees. In this situation, when employees will be directly affected by new policies, the superintendent should do a lot of listening and little talking.

Orchestrative. An orchestrative leader relates to employees in much the same way a conductor relates to the members of an orchestra. For this leadership style to be effective, all workers must be highly skilled at their jobs and motivated to work and succeed independently. They must also possess pride in their work. Highly competent and independent workers tend to prefer this leadership style. Orchestration is particularly suited to situations in which:

- skilled, experienced personnel can meet their responsibilities with complete confidence
- established policies and procedures allow you to delegate tasks and responsibilities comfortably
- problems are solved as a team

- a new supervisor who lacks experience in the company's day-to-day operations can gain from the experience and expertise of workers

A good time to call upon the orchestrative approach to leadership is during the peak of home production each year. During this hectic time when resources are spread thin, a superintendent may delegate some tasks, relying on the good judgment of employees to get through the busiest weeks of the year.

The Superintendent as Manager

As a superintendent, you are part of a management team. Therefore, you should be trained as a manager and supervisor and act primarily in that capacity. In too many companies, superintendents brought up through the trades are placed in supervisory positions without even the most basic management training. This lack of training can prove detrimental when novice superintendents suddenly find themselves overseeing production and quality control, rather than producing the work themselves. As a manager, your performance is measured by what others do. How well you motivate workers and subcontractors to produce is a key factor in your success.

People who study management often divide the topic into four basic elements: planning, organizing, directing, and controlling. The effective superintendent successfully applies all four of these elements to reach the three goals of bringing the job in on time, within the budget, and according to the quality standards established. By understanding these basics and applying them on your jobs, you can become a better superintendent.

Planning

Someone once summarized management planning in the following way:

"Plan your work, and work your plan."

Planning is the most basic and most important function of management, requiring that you simply figure out what must be done. When you plan, you develop a program of action to achieve stated goals through the use of people, materials, and financial resources. While you, as a superintendent, are responsible for planning all the activities that come under your direction, you also must implement the plans of the builder to whom you report. The saying "Proper planning prevents poor performance" holds especially true in the building industry. Problems arise when no overall objectives are established, when policies and programs conflict, or when procedures are wasteful or poorly thought out.

Many superintendents understand the need for planning, but have never really been taught what or how to plan. Bob Whitten, chief operating officer of Wayne Homes and former director of Business Management at NAHB, has developed an outline to guide superintendents in planning. With his permission, I have adapted it for use here.

Planning is a continuous process, but certain planning activities should be scheduled or reviewed regularly on a yearly, quarterly, monthly, weekly, or daily basis.

Yearly Planning. On a yearly basis, the superintendent should review, evaluate, and revise, as needed, the following:

- subcontract agreements
- performance of subcontractors and availability of subcontractors to establish a stable subcontractor base

- house quality checklist
- performance of in-house construction personnel
- projections of needs for in-house construction personnel, including training
- scheduling system
- internal and external communication systems
- annual forecast of sales, starts, and closings
- production policies and procedures
- managerial policies and procedures

Quarterly Planning. On a quarterly basis, the superintendent should monitor the status of and adjust, as needed, the following:

- all yearly items
- quarterly forecast of sales, starts, and closings
- potential material shortages and price increases
- accuracy of construction projections and schedules
- changes to production procedures

Monthly Planning (on a Projected Workload Basis). Monthly, according to projected workload, the superintendent should analyze and take steps to adjust, as needed, the following:

- subcontractor availability and scheduling
- recurring material and production problems

Weekly Planning (on a Unit-by-Unit Basis). Weekly, unit by unit, the superintendent should evaluate and adjust, as needed, the following:

- long-range weather forecast
- overall status of all active jobs
- starts and closings
- communications with homeowner
- meetings
- subcontractor schedules for the next three weeks
- delivery schedules
- inspection schedules
- critical places to be at specific times of the week

The superintendent must also be sure to communicate revised schedules to all concerned parties and analyze the long-range weather forecast to anticipate factors that may interfere with the schedules.

Daily Planning (on a Unit-by-Unit Basis).

Daily, the superintendent should review, verify, and adjust, *for each job*, the following:

- weather forecast for the immediate future to adjust schedules as necessary
- work to be accomplished today
- worksite readiness for next scheduled subcontractor
- material drop zones and sites (to be sure they are properly prepared and marked)
- daily communications with homeowners
- daily communications with subcontractors

The superintendent must also discuss relevant problems and corrective measures with the builder or other supervisors, communicate any last-minute schedule changes, and communicate with the homeowner if necessary. Because so many quick decisions occur each day on the jobsite, many superintendents use a daily "to do" list to help ensure that no critical decision or action is forgotten. Learning to prioritize tasks and handle unforeseen problems according to their impact is an important aspect of daily supervision.

Organizing

The tasks of planning and organizing work often overlap. Once you have determined what needs to be done during the planning stage, you must organize the job, determining who is going to perform the work and how completion of the task fits into the overall scheme.

The organization of work boils down to one question:

"Who does what by when?"

This simple formula is the key to getting things done. The *who* part of the question requires you to allocate personnel and other resources to accomplish the task. It also involves the establishment or use of lines of authority and responsibility to guide the assigned workers. *What* requires you to determine exactly which tasks will be performed. Finally, *when*—the phase of organization most often overlooked—must be carefully planned. Chapter 5 of this book explains how to schedule activities on the jobsite for maximum efficiency.

The "To Do" List

Trying to carry around a list of half a dozen tasks in your head takes up valuable storage space in your memory. One of the easiest yet most effective methods of planning involves maintaining a written list of all things to be done each day. In the past 10 years there has been a proliferation of time management systems, some manual and others computerized. These systems help you keep track of appointments as well as the things you need to accomplish each day. Many of the new computerized scheduling programs include a built-in, updatable list of tasks that need to be completed. Each day, you can generate and print a new list of critical tasks. The list is integrated with your activities on the schedule. For example, a day or so before you are scheduled to place the footings, the program reminds you to call in the inspection and place a "will call" for the concrete. Any items you don't complete are automatically carried over to the next day's list. These programs are marvelous management tools for the superintendent.

Your time management system can be as simple as a $15 day planner purchased at an office supply store or a $35 electronic pocket organizer, or as complex as a $4,000 fully integrated scheduling software package for your personal computer.

There are two additional organizational factors you must consider. The first is your own authority as a superintendent to organize workers to perform a certain task. The second is a clearly understood policy controlling hiring and firing, which will allow you to maximize your organizational efforts. For example, do you as a superintendent have the authority to fire a subcontractor for failure to comply with company policies or poor quality of work, or is this decision reserved for the company owner?

Directing and Coordinating

The majority of a superintendent's time is spent directing and coordinating tasks. Therefore, these efforts must be targeted directly at the primary goal. However, through better planning and organizing, you can be much more effective and get the most out of your limited amount of time. If planning is complete and your objectives are reasonable, all activities should contribute to achieving your goals, and any deviations can be corrected through effective control procedures. You should spend most of your time directing and coordinating those areas critical to company success. If a project progresses according to the plan, no additional directions are needed. As much as possible, handle routine matters through routine policies and procedures. Only extraordinary items falling beyond preset standards should require management attention. Of course, any deviations important to upper management should be reported to the builder or your superior in a daily or weekly report.

Controlling

Superintendents are directly involved in controlling activities. The scope of your activities may include control of materials, construction methods, labor, waste prevention, and costs. In addition, you will ordinarily have the authority to make decisions that affect the selection of subcontractors and the quantities and cost of labor used. In short, your job is to control events to conform to the plan you have already established, note any variances from the plan, and develop alternative plans to mitigate damages and get things back in line.

Superintendent Control System and Reports. Your entire control system should be economical—detailed enough to highlight deviations from your plans, yet not so detailed as to become burdensome or overly expensive. While complex controls can be extremely useful, they can become so complicated that they are rarely or never used. Therefore, your reports should be timely, but not time-consuming. Always keep in mind that management needs to keep up to date on job progress in order to make accurate, sound decisions. It will normally take about an hour each day to fill out and update the various reports required. Some of the common reports include the following:

- daily things-to-do reports
- updated schedules
- cost control variance reports
- customer service reports

- progress reports summarizing the status of each job and commitments made, usually in the form of a daily log

Accounting and Cost Control. Superintendents are also directly involved in controlling the cost of each construction project.

In order to track and report the financial status of each job accurately, accounting and bookkeeping personnel must be kept informed of cost-related activities. The superintendent's daily progress reports will provide much of this information. Accounting departments in larger companies may have their own forms that require you to fill in specific information. Whether you are filling in forms for an accounting department or simply handing progress reports to your builder, you should be careful to safeguard all financial information, sharing it only on a "need-to-know" basis and using it wisely.

The superintendent must carefully review supplier and subcontractor invoices and payments, purchase orders, and work orders. Work must be completed satisfactorily prior to authorization of payment. You should have a basic understanding of lien laws as they pertain to a builder's financial liability in order to prevent possible legal problems with subcontractors.

Construction Activities

A large part of your responsibilities as a superintendent will involve coordination of the basic elements of construction: materials, labor, equipment, subcontractors, customers, financial resources, and time. Each of these elements affects and is affected by the others. To coordinate these elements, you will need to develop a well-organized system that incorporates four essential activities: estimating, scheduling, staffing, and evaluation.

Estimating

Depending upon the company's size and organizational structure, estimating may be performed by staff estimators, the builder, the superintendent, or someone else in the company. Superintendents may not be asked to estimate jobs, but they are expected to build each job according to its estimate. Because you probably

How Much Do You Need to Know?

Builders have yet to agree on how much information to give superintendents. Some feel that much sensitive information should be held from superintendents. Pricing and cost information, for example, are often held in the strictest confidence. Builders who withhold this information avoid the risk that it will "leak out" and somehow be divulged to the competition.

Others feel that superintendents should be privy to almost all information, including financial information. They contend that the superintendent is a key person within the organization and, as such, needs the best and most accurate information available in order to manage effectively.

As a superintendent for two builders, I built well over 100 homes without being given any information concerning cost or even quantity of material with which to build them. Presumably, the builder did a good estimate of the home as part of the bidding process. However, that information was withheld from superintendents. To perform your job and contain costs adequately, you need to be aware of the expenditure of funds on each project in relation to the original budget. Superintendents need to have all of the information necessary in order to build the home, including cost information. In return, the builder must be able to trust the superintendent to keep sensitive information confidential.

know more about the actual construction process than anyone else involved, you can and should be an information source for the estimator, providing accurate, reliable information that will decrease the chances of estimating errors. At bare minimum, the superintendent should review the estimate to make sure it reflects the materials and methods which will be used in the construction of the project. Review of a typical estimate normally requires at least two to three hours, and complex jobs may require much longer. Chapter 2 provides a more detailed list of key items the superintendent must review.

Scheduling

Scheduling is one of the primary duties of the superintendent. Together with the builder, the superintendent should select a scheduling system appropriate for the company. You may use the critical path method (CPM), a bar chart, a time line, or some other form of scheduling. As the superintendent, you will ultimately be responsible for employee and subcontractor deadlines, so you should be actively involved in determining who does what in which order and when. It is your responsibility to evaluate alternatives, establish contingency plans, and make sure that employees and subcontractors are scheduled in an optimum manner. The overall schedule needs to be developed within the guidelines of your company policies.

Developing a schedule for an average house normally requires from one to four hours, depending on the size and complexity of the house and the level of detail in the schedule. The scheduling method you use also depends to a large degree on the number of concurrent projects you will supervise. For example, if you are responsible for multiple projects, you are more likely to make use of computerized scheduling programs. Once the schedule is established, you are also responsible for enforcing it, seeing to it that the work progresses smoothly and is done to the builder's satisfaction. You should expect to spend about 15 to 30 minutes per day updating the schedule. Scheduling methods and techniques will be discussed in more detail in Chapter 5.

Staffing

Most superintendents have the authority to hire and fire in-house construction personnel and subcontractors. In addition, you may be responsible for training all site personnel and subcontractors regarding acceptable quality standards, operating procedures, construction methods, production efficiency, and company policies and procedures. Larger building firms may hire safety training managers to instruct employees on safety issues and OSHA compliance, while smaller builders delegate this responsibility to the superintendent. Training employees and subcontractors is an ongoing process. If you use the same subcontractors on a consistent basis, your training responsibilities can be streamlined to some extent. If you use many different subcontractors or experience a period of high turnover in in-house personnel, you will need to devote more time and energy to training. In many ways you are like a teacher or an athletic coach; you must continually go back and cover basics as you bring your people along.

Evaluation

Industry experts in many businesses frequently say, "Superior managers get superior results."

As a member of the management team, you receive part of the credit for building a profitable, growing business. Your performance as a superintendent should therefore be evaluated regularly according to previously established objectives. Figure 1.2 presents a self-evaluation form that will help you measure your progress and guide you in upgrading your performance. If you find you are weak in some areas, you can work to improve your skills by reading, formal training, or education, and consultation and conversation with other superintendents and builders.

Figure 1.2 Superintendent's Self-Evaluation

Rate yourself as to your strengths and weaknesses.

	Always	Sometimes	Occasionally	Never
I schedule my own time and the time of others appropriately.	❑	❑	❑	❑
I am able to accomplish all of the important things each day.	❑	❑	❑	❑
I develop a schedule for each project before it begins.	❑	❑	❑	❑
I am aware of the status of all important aspects of the jobs.	❑	❑	❑	❑
I update construction schedules regularly.	❑	❑	❑	❑
I motivate others to do the designated amount of work in the designated time.	❑	❑	❑	❑
I complete projects on time.	❑	❑	❑	❑

Cost control

	Always	Sometimes	Occasionally	Never
I establish a budget before construction begins on each individual project.	❑	❑	❑	❑
I am cost-conscious.	❑	❑	❑	❑
I control costs discretely.	❑	❑	❑	❑
I foster cost-consciousness in others.	❑	❑	❑	❑
I prepare material use or cut sheets.	❑	❑	❑	❑
I update the budget and calculate the cost variance regularly.	❑	❑	❑	❑
I identify the causes of cost variances properly and eliminate negative variances regularly.	❑	❑	❑	❑
I follow a systematic purchase order system.	❑	❑	❑	❑
I keep accurate records of all change orders.	❑	❑	❑	❑
I see that materials are properly stored in appropriate material storage areas on the jobsite.	❑	❑	❑	❑
I control waste.	❑	❑	❑	❑
I see that tools and equipment are properly taken care of.	❑	❑	❑	❑

Quality Control

	Always	Sometimes	Occasionally	Never
I have well-defined quality standards established for each project.	❑	❑	❑	❑

Figure 1.2 Superintendent's Self-Evaluation (continued)

	Always	Sometimes	Occasionally	Never
I communicate quality standards to each subcontractor, supplier, and worker.	❑	❑	❑	❑
I conduct systematic quality control inspections.	❑	❑	❑	❑
I am respectful of customers and responsive to their needs.	❑	❑	❑	❑
I control the quality of work performed on my projects.	❑	❑	❑	❑
I schedule and monitor the necessary inspections.	❑	❑	❑	❑

Safety

	Always	Sometimes	Occasionally	Never
I am safety conscious.	❑	❑	❑	❑
I display a knowledge of both company and governmental (OSHA) safety and health rules and regulations.	❑	❑	❑	❑
I follow the company safety program religiously.	❑	❑	❑	❑
I correct safety problems promptly.	❑	❑	❑	❑
I am aware of HazCom Standards and ensure that they are followed on my jobs.	❑	❑	❑	❑
I keep my jobsites clean.	❑	❑	❑	❑

Organization

	Always	Sometimes	Occasionally	Never
I have an appearance of organization.	❑	❑	❑	❑
I get results by organization of paperwork.	❑	❑	❑	❑
My desk/truck is organized.	❑	❑	❑	❑

Delegation of duties

	Always	Sometimes	Occasionally	Never
I delegate duties appropriately.	❑	❑	❑	❑
I assume responsibilities for those duties that I delegate.	❑	❑	❑	❑
I follow the lines of authority, as a supervisor and a subordinate.	❑	❑	❑	❑
I work well under pressure.	❑	❑	❑	❑
I maintain self-control.	❑	❑	❑	❑
I control the situation rather than permit the situation to control me.	❑	❑	❑	❑

Management concepts

	Always	Sometimes	Occasionally	Never
I spend the necessary time planning.	❑	❑	❑	❑
I avoid management by crisis.	❑	❑	❑	❑
I set objectives.	❑	❑	❑	❑
I establish a plan to achieve the objectives.	❑	❑	❑	❑
I set major limitations and controls.	❑	❑	❑	❑
I measure my own performance as well as the performance of others on the basis of previously established objectives.	❑	❑	❑	❑
I delay decision making until I have investigated the answers.	❑	❑	❑	❑
I keep adequate daily records on each individual job.	❑	❑	❑	❑
I ensure that records are adequate enough to cover essential elements but not cumbersome or time-consuming.	❑	❑	❑	❑
Subcontractors and suppliers enjoy working with me.	❑	❑	❑	❑
I coordinate all the essential elements of construction, including the performance of subs, suppliers, and others.	❑	❑	❑	❑

Figure 1.2 Superintendent's Self-Evaluation (continued)

	Always	Sometimes	Occasionally	Never
Computers				
I am computer literate.	❏	❏	❏	❏
I use the following computer programs proficiently:				
word processing.	❏	❏	❏	❏
spreadsheets.	❏	❏	❏	❏
construction estimating.	❏	❏	❏	❏
construction scheduling.	❏	❏	❏	❏
cost control systems.	❏	❏	❏	❏
Interpersonal Performance				
I help establish performance goals for others.	❏	❏	❏	❏
I evaluate the performance of others on the basis of these goals.	❏	❏	❏	❏
I receive cooperation from others.	❏	❏	❏	❏
I am respected.	❏	❏	❏	❏
Training of others				
I encourage training and establish the means for it.	❏	❏	❏	❏
I motivate others to perform their maximum potential.	❏	❏	❏	❏
I have the courage and fortitude for hiring and firing.	❏	❏	❏	❏
I measure my own performance based upon the improvement of others.	❏	❏	❏	❏
My performance appraisal standards are objective.	❏	❏	❏	❏
I listen effectively, to both subordinates and superiors.	❏	❏	❏	❏
I reward superior performance:	❏	❏	❏	❏
with praise.	❏	❏	❏	❏
with consideration.	❏	❏	❏	❏
with monetary means.	❏	❏	❏	❏
with other types of remuneration.	❏	❏	❏	❏
I communicate or carry out requests of both subordinates and superiors.	❏	❏	❏	❏
I let others carry out their responsibility.	❏	❏	❏	❏
I step in and take over for others when it is necessary without adversely affecting their morale.	❏	❏	❏	❏
Personal				
I display a lot of common sense.	❏	❏	❏	❏
I have good people skills.	❏	❏	❏	❏
I display a positive attitude.	❏	❏	❏	❏
I set goals for myself.	❏	❏	❏	❏
I seek self-improvement through seminars, study, schooling, consultations with others, or other means.	❏	❏	❏	❏
I display the ability to become more of an asset to the organization.	❏	❏	❏	❏

Chapter 2

Project Start-Up

Introduction

As the company's field representative, your primary responsibility is to control and manage the projects in three areas: cost, schedule, and quality. Therefore, you must effectively and conscientiously administer a construction program to meet the primary objective of maximizing profits and quality standards while you maintain good business relationships with suppliers, subcontractors, inspectors, and others. As the superintendent, you must bring all available resources to bear upon the timely, cost-effective completion of the project. An effective, conscientious superintendent with the necessary authority and resources can exercise careful control, decrease costs, meet tight schedules, and ensure high-quality work. Without the necessary authority and resources, however, the inevitable result is loss of control, increased costs, prolonged schedules, and poor quality.

Starting Off Right

A project that starts off right has a much better chance of finishing up successfully. On the other hand, a project that starts off on the wrong foot may be doomed from the beginning. Too often, homes are built with little forethought and planning. New superintendents may be tempted to start off assuming they will plan as they go. Such superintendents are likely to have big problems when subcontractors fail to show up or arrive to find the previous sub not finished and still working on the job. If lumber and other materials are not delivered to the jobsite in a timely manner, two conflicting subs can end up working in the same area.

Planning

If you want a job to turn out right, you have to spend the time planning up front. The key is to get ahead of the details and stay ahead as the project progresses. If you allow the job to start before you are ready, you will have difficulty regaining control of it. Far too often, the job takes on a life of its own and ends up managing itself *and the superintendent*. The superintendent must then spend too much time, money, and energy putting out fires that should never have started in the first place.

You can ensure that your jobs start off right with good preliminary planning and scheduling. Planning prior to the start of construction will free up time later, when the construction process demands much of your attention.

Construction Documents

To meet responsibilities, every superintendent must be familiar with the company's construction documents and those specific for each job, including the plans, specifications, and each subcontract agreement. You should have a basic understanding of construction contract law. In addition, you will want to be familiar with all the requirements of an enforceable contract, including the following:

- homeowner (buyer) responsibilities
- scope of work
- price
- schedule requirements
- delivery of materials and supplies
- payment provisions
- lien laws
- liquidated damages, if any
- termination of subcontractors

- change orders
- contract interpretation

Preconstruction

The superintendent acts as the catalyst for the preconstruction activities that bring the whole building process together. Other people may be involved, but the superintendent should be the leader. Key elements in the successful planning of preconstruction activities include:

- plans
- specifications
- buyer prequalification
- lot inspection
- customizing the home to the lot
- material and color selections
- plan review with homeowner
- homeowner preconstruction conference
- plan review by superintendent
- cost estimate
- identification of key personnel, subcontractors, and suppliers to be used on the project
- discussion of special requirements or administrative procedures that are unique to the job with key personnel, subs, and suppliers
- plan review with key personnel, including review of the specifications
- review of initial estimate and purchase orders
- release of purchase orders
- securing of required permits
- establishment of start date
- hookup of temporary power

Lot Inspection

One of the first things you must do before building is make sure that the lot and the home fit together. If you are building a straight ranch-style home, it is helpful to have a fairly flat lot. If you are building a home with a drive-under garage, it is nice to have a lot with a fair amount of slope. Flat lots and hillside lots require different planning. A lot in the country where a well and septic system are required has entirely different planning needs from a lot in the city.

As the company's jobsite supervisor, the superintendent is normally responsible for evaluating site considerations relating to the job. For example, he or she may be called upon to evalu-

ate conditions such as high water tables, unique drainage or excavation requirements, or areas where the slope or soil conditions of the lot do not permit building a home according to the plan. The superintendent is usually the best resource for resolving onsite problems. The following items should be considered during a lot inspection (Normally, the information from the lot inspection is recorded on the plot plan.):

- location of property pins
- location of the home on the lot, including setbacks
- tree removal and clearing
- location and size of driveway
- location, size, and depth of utility trenches (water, electrical, gas, sewer, and cable TV)
- location of power meter base and circuit breaker box
- location of temporary power and water
- establishment of existing grades and final grades in relationship to the house
- removal and stockpiling of topsoil as appropriate
- need for additional fill or existence of excess excavated material
- house drainage, where applicable (footing sump system, natural drain)
- subsoil conditions (water table and rock) for homes with basements
- location of well and septic system in rural areas
- location of air conditioner or heat pump
- most feasible method of trash disposal

Many builders bring the customer to the site for a lot inspection prior to the preconstruction meeting. The superintendent meets with the customer after the plans have been drawn and customized for the home. He or she conducts a complete lot inspection and lays out the lot, locating the utility trenches and lines. While the buyer is on the lot, the superintendent reviews the house plans in detail to make sure that everyone understands how it will fit on the lot. The superintendent draws a detailed plot plan of the lot, a cross-section of the house showing existing grade and projected final grade, and an excavation plan (dig plan) of the house. The superintendent reviews the plans, particularly the foundation plan, to locate the furnace, water heater, sump pump or natural drainage system, and other plumbing fixtures, including the soil pipe exit.

Project and Site Logistics

In addition to being responsible for—and taking direct charge of—site layout, superintendents should also be concerned with such site logistics as access, water, electrical lines, and others. The lot inspection checklists in Figure 2.1 will give you a model to use during a site visit.

Arrange for Utilities. Utilities must be made readily available so that subcontractors and other workers do not have to waste time stringing extension cords great distances in order to obtain power or run long hoses to obtain water. Contact utility companies prior to the start of construction to arrange for temporary hookups at the jobsite. Temporary utility service at each jobsite will allow for specific job cost expense allocations.

Organize the Physical Layout. Each home should have a site plan indicating location of the home, temporary power, water, trash disposal, culinary water trench or well, lateral sewers or septic system, and so forth. Laying out the site on most large custom-built homes involves the efficient placement of a storage area, perhaps a jobsite office, and areas for fabrication, if required. The objective of an effective physical layout is to ensure that work can be performed efficiently. Every physical site has its own special set of conditions that make this layout unique. For example, your requirements for a cramped urban subdivision or multifamily site will be much different from those for a rural location.

On scattered sites, a pickup truck and cellular phone may be the only "office" available. In some cases, a temporary field office and storage shed may be warranted. Your field office may be nothing more than a portable shed or designated area containing a small desk or plan table and a telephone. On a large project, a field office can be a particularly effective time saver, giving the superintendent a central location from which to control the project. A storage area should be located where it will not interfere with other

activities, yet still be as close as possible to the areas where the stored materials will be used.

Prepare for Surface Water Control. Once started, grading should be completed as quickly as possible to minimize continuing disturbance of the soil. Open trenches should be covered as soon as possible. Make sure that straw bales or silt fences are ready for use in controlling and filtering runoff; rock or gravel may also be needed for filtering. Consider using temporary collecting ponds in the event of unforeseen, severe wet weather.

Preconstruction Meetings

One management tool that has been used almost universally in commercial construction and is being adopted more frequently in residential construction is the preconstruction conference. A preconstruction meeting can significantly improve relationships with clients and give them the confidence that you are the right builder for them. The primary purpose of the preconstruction conference is to set the expectation levels of all of the major participants in the project. The superintendent, homeowners, key subcontractors, suppliers, and others may attend as necessary, including representatives from the power company and health department (in rural areas where well and septic systems are required). The meeting typically covers a company's normal policies and procedures for managing a project, written copies of which are often distributed to the homeowner and each of the key participants in the project. The homeowner, who was given a copy of the company's warranty agreement at the time of the purchase agreement, may be asked to review the warranty and sign it during the preconstruction meeting. The discussion may also include manufacturers' warranties on items such as roofing, siding, windows, cabinets, and so forth. Because most residential builders use the same subcontractors and suppliers over and over again, most of these subs and suppliers soon become familiar with the project policies and procedures. For a production home builder, therefore, it may be necessary to include only new subs or suppliers in the preconstruction conference. For a custom builder who uses unique subcontractors for each

Figure 2.1 Lot Inspection Checklist

Job number: _____   Name: _____   Date: _____

Home phone: _____   Business/work phone: _____

Model of house: _____   Garage on: Left ❑ Right ❑

Job address: Street and lot number: _____

City: _____   County: _____   Township: _____

Lot size: _____   Set back: _____ft.   From: _____

Sidelines seen from street: Left _____ ft.   Right _____ft.

Part I

Explain and check either yes or no

	Yes	No		Yes	No
Lot previously filled	❑	❑	Change order from lot		
Property pins located	❑	❑	inspection	❑	❑
Owner pre-wire phone/TV	❑	❑	Zoning permit	❑	❑
Easements/restriction	❑	❑	Remove dirt from drive	❑	❑
Review contract	❑	❑	Additional excavation or		
Discuss change orders	❑	❑	cut swale	❑	❑
Discuss allowances	❑	❑	Drive/permit/culvert	❑	❑
Trash and cleanup	❑	❑	Clear lot, stumps, trees	❑	❑
Temporary downspout lines	❑	❑	No move-in until closing	❑	❑
Garage floor elevation	❑	❑	Recommend change location	❑	❑
Whom and when owner should			Electric for well & septic	❑	❑
call for information	❑	❑	Flood zone	❑	❑
Building specifications	❑	❑			
Homeowner's responsibilities					
list	❑	❑			

Special comments:

_____

_____

_____

_____

_____

_____

Homeowner signature: _____   Date: _____

Figure 2.1 Lot Inspection Checklist (continued)

Part II

Utilities

Electric company: _____   100 amp ❑ 200 amp ❑

Service location: _____   overhead ❑ underground ❑

Application made: yes ❑ no ❑
Temp. pole: yes ❑ no ❑   100 amp ❑ 200 amp❑   overhead ❑ underground ❑

Panel location: _____

Mast pipe: yes ❑ no ❑   Displaced service: yes ❑ no ❑   Rope service: yes ❑ no ❑
Underground service by: homeowner ❑ electric company ❑

Sewer location: _____   Sewer depth: _____

Septic location: _____   Type of system: _____

Soil exit: _____   Through: footer ❑ foundation wall ❑

Electric circuit needed for septic system: yes ❑ no ❑   Supplied by: homeowner ❑ W/H ❑

City water: yes ❑ no ❑   Well: yes ❑ no ❑

Location of water line into house: _____

Location of pressure tank:

_____

Pressure regulator required: ❑ yes ❑ no

Circuit for well needed: yes ❑ no ❑   homeowner ❑ builder ❑

Natural gas: yes ❑ no ❑   Name of company: _____

Application made: yes ❑ no ❑

Length of exterior gas line: _____   Size of exterior gas line: _____

Liquid propane: yes ❑ no ❑   Location of tank: _____

Length of interior gas line: _____   Size of interior gas line: _____

Location of gas line exit: _____

Footer sump: yes ❑ no ❑   Laundry sump: yes ❑ no ❑
Natural footer drain: yes ❑ no ❑   Length: _____

(continued)

Figure 2.1 Lot Inspection Checklist (continued)

Extra fill needed: yes ❑ no ❑   Location: _____

Type of fill: _____   Supplied by: homeowner ❑ builder ❑

Extra block needed: yes ❑ no ❑ maybe ❑   Amount: _____

Homeowner signature: _____   Date: _____

Part III

Superintendent

Indicate on print:

- ❑ Present grade
- ❑ Finish grade
- ❑ Extra block
- ❑ Footer sump location
- ❑ Laundry sump location
- ❑ Water line location
- ❑ Pressure tank location
- ❑ Soil exit
- ❑ Electric service
- ❑ Electric panel
- ❑ Gas line exit
- ❑ Washer & dryer
- ❑ A/C or heat pump location

Indicate on plot plan:

- ❑ House location (set backs)
- ❑ Temporary pole
- ❑ All elevations
- ❑ Measurements
- ❑ Existing structures
- ❑ Propane tank
- ❑ All utilities
- ❑ Natural drain
- ❑ Drive

- ❑ Stake temporary pole
- ❑ Post builder's sign

Special comments:

_____

_____

_____

_____

_____

_____

Superintendent's signature: _____   Date: _____

job, it may be necessary to have them attend the preconstruction conference for each job. Either way, a preconstruction conference with the homeowner will be very helpful. This meeting may be conducted by the superintendent, the production manager, the sales manager, or others as the case may be.

The timing of the preconstruction meeting varies. Some builders hold the meeting immediately following the lot inspection. Others wait a few days. The meeting itself can take 2 to 4 hours. The objective of the preconstruction meeting is to establish the responsibilities and expectations of each participant. Lines of communication must be established among all participants, including both the regular channels of authority and communication procedures for the items listed below:

- color selections
- construction schedules
- materials and methods to be employed
- acceptance of work
- inspections
- change orders
- safety
- payment
- disputes
- builder's and manufacturers' warranties and procedures
- insurance coverage
- permits and fees
- allowances
- bank draws
- location and makeup of driveway
- appliances
- HVAC systems and alternatives
- utility hookup
- trash disposal
- painting and decorating
- floor coverings
- homeowner's responsibilities
- grading and drainage away from the home
- communication

On smaller jobs or for production housing, when a formal preconstruction meeting is deemed unnecessary, the superintendent should meet with all project participants individually and cover the necessary information.

Planning the Preconstruction Meeting.
Proper planning can ensure that meeting time is more productive for everyone. You should prepare an itemized agenda or checklist of items to be discussed and distribute it to participants so that they can reserve questions or comments until the appropriate time. The meeting should be conveniently located and held in a comfortable place that is conducive to a successful meeting.

Conducting the Meeting.
When conducting a preconstruction meeting, you should:

- take minutes yourself or be sure that a person present takes minutes
- begin on time and maintain control of the meeting
- establish ground rules
- define items to be discussed
- stick to the agenda
- obtain scheduling commitments from subcontractors (where applicable)
- solve problems
- summarize decisions made
- solicit questions and feedback from all participants
- set time aside for questions and answers

During the meeting, you will also want to examine and discuss the construction schedule and point out critical dates for delivery of materials and completion of various phases of the project. Subcontractors should also receive tentative dates for start-up of their work. They should discuss the schedule and resolve any conflicts that may exist. In addition, you should solicit a commitment from each subcontractor and supplier to comply with the schedule *as agreed upon.* Penalties for noncompliance should then be clearly defined and established. At this time, you should outline each individual's responsibility with regard to customer call-backs and warranties, and establish a procedure for problem solving. The superintendent and subcontractors should establish who will be responsible for calling in which inspections. Finally, minutes of the meeting should be distributed to all participants. Figure 2.2 provides an example of a preconstruction meeting agenda.

Figure 2.2 Preconstruction Meeting Agenda

Review all items with each homeowner prior to the start of construction. If an item does not pertain to the homeowner, mark it "N/A" (not applicable). After the review is complete, have the homeowner sign and date any pertinent document. You may give a copy to the homeowners if they request one.

Items Needed for Review:

Sales Contract—Review sales contract to make sure all necessary information is correct. Items may include required insurance coverage, responsibility for utility bills, and procedures for allowances.

Plans—Go over the blueprint of the home in detail. Discuss dimensions, traffic patterns, location of appliances, light switches, and outlets, which areas will be finished or unfinished, and any other details that might cause confusion or might not be fully understood. Note any changes required on the plans.

Specifications—Make sure specifications are included in the file and review with the homeowner any questions about the methods and materials to be used in the construction process. Review construction draw schedules. Check for all required signatures and dates. Make sure that the homeowner has a set of specifications and that you have a signed copy.

Change Orders—Review the change orders already in the file. Make sure that all change orders, however minor, are completed and signed. Have a change order form to fill out in case there are any changes as a result of the decisions made at the preconstruction conference.

Permits—Discuss the acquisition of the necessary permits including the building permit and the payment of fees. Discuss the role of the homeowner in this process.

Lot Inspection Sheets—Make sure the lot inspection sheets are in the file and that they are properly filled out. Explain plans for finish grade, drainage, etc. Write change orders as needed for any extra grading, fill, etc., known at this time. Ask the homeowners if they have any questions as a result of the lot inspection.

Utilities—Discuss the location and availability of utilities both temporary and permanent, and review the homeowner's responsibilities relating to applications or installation.

Site Plan—Briefly review the site plan and make sure the home is properly located. Discuss potential problems inherent or unique to the site, such as drainage, location of septic system and utility lines, potential interference between construction operations and existing trees, etc. Review the homeowner's future plans for adding a pool, deck, or other features.

Color Selection Sheets—Assist the homeowner in making color selections and in selecting cabinets, appliances, etc. Check the color selection sheets to make sure they are filled out. Be sure any special items that may not be on the standard sheet are also covered. Make sure that the homeowners understand the importance of timely decisions regarding items such as lighting fixtures, paint, and wall coverings. Check to be sure color selection sheets are signed and dated by the homeowners.

Floor Coverings—Discuss in detail who will be responsible for which floor coverings and when they will be installed. If the builder will handle floor coverings, make sure that the carpet selection sheet is completed and signed.

Construction Schedule—Review the construction schedule with the homeowners. Discuss sequence of activities and the superintendent workload, and review protocol for phone calls (when and how). Emphasize that your schedule will vary due to factors such as weather and inspections.

Walk-Through—Briefly discuss the homeowners' walk-through.

Closing Package—Discuss the closing process and the homeowners' role in it. When keys are given to the homeowners, discuss credits and charges that will appear on closing sheet, monies to be paid at closing, emergency phone numbers, and any other particulars.

Warranty and Service—Discuss the warranty service policies and procedures. Note the difference between warranties covered by the builder and warranties from equipment manufacturers.

Identifying Problems. Part of the purpose of the preconstruction meeting is to identify potential issues and problems. As problems come up during the course of the preconstruction meeting, keep your mind open to the alternatives and solutions suggested. Discussing problems without proposing or accepting viable solutions wastes time (unless further information is required). Methods of carrying out solutions, measuring results, and reporting back to the group must be established.

Schedules

The construction schedule will dictate the sequence of construction: Which activities must follow one another? For example, if the interior trim is to be stained, it may be best to stain the trim and paint the interior walls before the trim is installed. However, if the trim is to be painted, then it would be more efficient to install the trim before painting.

Deliveries need to be scheduled so that materials are available when needed, but not so early that they take up valuable storage space for an excessively long time—or disappear before they are used. Workers should not have to move materials to accommodate or avoid subcontractors. Through planning and careful scheduling, such conflicts can be avoided.

Regulations

Superintendents should always keep informed of local ordinances and regulations pertaining to their jobs and make certain to obtain all necessary permits. Discussing how best to comply with regulations, policies, and procedures with local building code officials will help you avoid problems at inspection time. Failure to comply with any regulation can mean considerable delays and, in some cases, fines for the builder. Inspectors may also require that perfectly good work be torn out if the necessary requirements are not met.

Defining Subcontractor Responsibilities

One of the superintendent's first responsibilities on a project is taking bids on work to be subcontracted and awarding the subcontracts.

Pre-Bid Procedures. Prior to receiving subcontractor bids, you must also determine how much each area of work should cost to assist in bid evaluation. When requesting bids, you should control subcontractor overlap and prevent gaps from occurring by clarifying and defining the exact scope of each subcontract or agreement. You might also arrange to have work not adequately described in the contract documents included as part of a specific subcontractor's agreement. For example, does the footing subcontractor lay out the foundation on the footings, or is that job someone else's responsibility? Does the framer install felt paper on the roof, or is that job performed by the roofing subcontractor? You will also want to determine who is responsible for cleanup of subcontractor operations and removal of trash from the jobsite. These responsibilities must be clarified in order for construction to flow smoothly.

Bid Review and Selection. With this information in hand, you can proceed with bid review and the issuing of subcontracts and major purchase orders. If authorized, you should participate in evaluating all bids and awarding the contracts to the various subcontractors. In some companies, this part of the process may be reserved exclusively for the builder. However, if you are going to be responsible for subcontractor coordination, you should also lend a hand to ensure that each subcontractor understands the line of authority and your position of responsibility.

Other Responsibilities. As the field superintendent, you will serve as a resource for the subcontractor, answering questions, clarifying instructions, and solving problems. In addition, you will be responsible for ensuring that all necessary equipment is safe, adequately maintained, and available to those who will be using it. Necessary accessories such as oil, saw blades, and power cords should be included.

Construction

A superintendent's administrative responsibilities do not end with preconstruction. A well-implemented system of documentation can make job control easier during construction and leave a valuable paper trail for each project.

Reports and Documents

Superintendents sometimes attempt to control a project with little more than a vague recollection of past performance on other projects. "Seat of the pants" management is a major cause of poor control on a construction project, and poor reporting practices are usually a large contributor. On the other hand, you may often find yourself deluged with more information than you can possibly use in controlling the project. A balance between these two extremes would allow you to obtain the exact level of detail and amount of information required.

Effective documents and reports can provide just such a balance. Reports documenting what actually occurred on a project can do the following:

- inform company management of project status at any given time
- establish projections of future activities
- assist in job control

Adequate documentation is also necessary in requesting change orders. Without proper documentation, pricing change orders and requesting payment for items beyond the scope of the contract are impossible.

Accuracy. In order for construction documents and reports to have any legal credibility, they must be accurate. Superintendents should be careful to note any specific details immediately to ensure the accuracy of all documented information.

Completeness. The superintendent must make certain that reports contain all information needed to manage and control the job properly. While remembering everything that happened on a construction job is impossible, you should document in writing any important occurrences at the time they occur. Some superintendents carry a pad of paper or notebook and are continually jotting down items they need to remember. Others carry a small tape recorder

to eliminate confusion and the time involved in writing, having the information transcribed later.

Objectivity. Reports must be objective to be acceptable. Facts should be presented without interjecting opinions. The credibility of a blatantly biased report may be called into question if litigation arises.

Uniformity. Reports should be provided on a standardized form or in a standardized format, facilitating comparisons with previous reports. Several samples of useful construction reports are found in Chapter 3, Quality Control and Inspections.

Believability. By documenting all necessary items in a timely and unbiased manner, you establish credibility as a superintendent. Most people can readily discern an altered or biased report. Handwritten reports are generally more acceptable in legal proceedings when they are documented and bound in such a way that pages cannot be moved or added. Original notes should never be modified; if something is forgotten and remembered later, add this information to another report at a later date rather than alter an earlier report to put the information in its "proper" place.

Timeliness. Timely reports are one of the key elements in improving communications and eliminating misunderstandings. To effectively manage and make informed decisions, reports must be completed regularly and kept as up to date as possible.

Types of Reports

Carefully maintained reports documenting daily activities and long-term project status can be important tools for the superintendent, the builder, and the customer.

Daily Reports. The daily report or activities log on the jobsite (see Figures 2.3 and 2.4) is generally a handwritten account, preferably in a bound book. Daily reports have greater legal credibility than nearly all other accounts of job activity. Therefore, you must maintain these reports accurately, including *all* items of importance, particularly any item that might become the subject of a disagreement.

Figure 2.3 Items to Include in the Daily Report

(Items to be included in the daily report need not be limited to this list.)

Job Conditions

- a complete description of the weather for the day including both high and low temperatures, in as much detail as necessary to document delays caused by weather
- any problems that arise related to utilities, access to the site, drainage, snow removal, and anything related to site conditions and facilities
- all visitors to the jobsite who are not directly involved in the construction process, such as inspectors, owners, architects, building officials, safety inspectors, government officials

Activities

- information received from the owner or design professional, including the selection of items, colors, change orders, and accessories
- work started, completed, or in progress
- labor problems, including disputes or disagreements
- all accidents (no matter how minor), including who was involved, witnesses, the circumstances surrounding the accident, the results, and any implications for safety authorities
- major material deliveries or delays
- purchase orders issued from the field or material purchased

Subcontractors

- subcontractors who start or complete work and work in progress

- the work force of each subcontractor on the job and major changes in the job
- questions to and from subcontractors
- instructions to subcontractors (follow up with memorandums)
- any disagreements with subcontractors or suppliers on the jobsite

Communications

- all change orders requested and the status of each change
- directives given by owners, inspectors, the builder, or architect
- any unusual circumstances or problems encountered as a result of these directives

Schedule

- work completed
- work in progress
- work to be started in the immediate future
- problems that relate to the schedule

Equipment

- all equipment present on the jobsite that day
- equipment needs
- rentals and returns
- breakdown and repairs
- other equipment problems

Contacts

- all phone conversations or personal contacts, the circumstances of each conversation, and the results

---

Daily reports have four basic purposes:

- to provide a record of activities
- to make immediate note of instructions given orally to ensure that action is taken and that the action is justified
- to back up future change order requests and additional charges
- for possible use in any dispute settlements, arbitration, or lawsuits

Progress Reports. These reports summarize the status of each phase of the project (see Figure

2.5). They perform the following functions for project managers and builders:

- communicate project status to company management and others
- summarize information contained in daily logs
- outline instructions and decisions made regarding subcontractors and suppliers
- summarize progress compared with the schedule
- allow coordination between the office and project superintendent by assembling the information in an organized fashion

Figure 2.4 Daily Report

Project: _____

Weather: ❑ fair ❑ overcast ❑ rain ❑ snow

Temperature: ❑ 0-50 ❑ 50-80 ❑ 80+

Job number: _____

Superintendent: _____

Wind: ❑ still ❑ moderate ❑ high

Work force/subcontractors

_____ Foreman	_____ Plumbers	_____ Bricklayers	_____ Cement finishers
_____ Foundation	_____ Electricians	_____ Roofers	_____ Floor covering installers
_____ Framers	_____ HVAC	_____ Tile installers	_____ (Other)
_____ Carpenters	_____ Insulators	_____ Painters	_____ (Other)
_____ Laborers	_____ Drywallers	_____ Cabinetmakers	_____ (Other)

Equipment on job: _____

_____

Remarks: _____

_____

Visitors

Time	Name	Representing	Remarks
_____	_____	_____	_____
_____	_____	_____	_____
_____	_____	_____	_____
_____	_____	_____	_____

Equipment needs, rentals, problems: _____

_____

Work completed (describe): _____

_____

Work in progress (describe): _____

_____

Remarks, phone conversations, contacts, problems: _____

Work in progress (describe status): _____

Superintendent's signature: _____ Date: _____

The progress report and the daily report should complement each other, with the progress report summarizing the daily report and communicating this necessary information to those involved in the project. Progress reports may be sent to subcontractors, suppliers, the homeowner, and the design professional.

Safety

Safety and health are as much a part of project planning and control as any other aspect of construction. As the superintendent, you are primarily responsible for ensuring that construction workers have a safe and healthy place in which to work, a responsibility mandated by law and required by government regulations. The Occupational Safety and Health Act, federal legislation dealing with safety and health in the construction industry, was an effort on the part of Congress to establish uniform standards throughout all industries to ensure and mandate adequate safety on the job.

Safety on the job must begin with the individuals working on the site. Workers should begin each project with the belief that safety on the job is a personal concern as well as the concern of every other worker on the project. Each worker should therefore be aware of safety hazards and avoid or correct them regardless of the existence of rules and regulations to eliminate them. However, because workers often fail in this most basic form of safety management, builders and contractors must establish their own safety rules and programs.

The Dangers of the Construction Site. The construction industry has traditionally been a difficult industry in which to work. At times, work is performed under adverse weather conditions and involves the use of hazardous materials, tools, and equipment. Other hazards include noise, dust, and explosions, as well as the potential threat of falling or being struck by falling material and equipment. Resulting injuries can prove catastrophic in terms of loss of life and personal injury.

Liability Problems. The recent tendency of the courts toward larger and larger settlements for parties injured as a result of inadequate protection on the job is alarming. Superintendents

and their building companies must establish an atmosphere of safety and become conscious of possible violations or unsafe conditions on the job.

Organizational Image. Any building company's public image can be seriously damaged or even destroyed by a single accident resulting from careless and unsafe conditions on a jobsite. It can prove almost impossible for a builder to live down the poor reputation resulting from a needless fatality due to an unsafe condition. In addition, the adverse publicity can be devastating. For example, at one construction site, a 5-year-old boy drowned in a hole dug for a septic tank. The resulting lawsuit and negative publicity were factors in the construction com-

---

Figure 2.5 Items to Include in a Progress Report

Communication to the Homeowner

- decisions and action required from the owner
- delays experienced and their causes
- oral instructions and information received from the owner
- change order requests and their status

Information for Subcontractors and Suppliers

- the status of each contract or major purchase order
- summary of instructions and changes occurring during the week
- items requiring coordination in current work
- notice of future performance requirements or schedule changes

Schedule Progress

- summary of the status of the schedule (as nearly as possible)
- comparison of the current status with the scheduled status of the project
- outline of any variances
- description of the impact of homeowner-caused delays on the project

Problems

- summary of problems, their apparent causes, and proposed solutions

pany's later declaration of bankruptcy. When a fatality is involved this result is not uncommon, and the personal grief suffered by persons who are witness to or involved in a fatal accident never truly ceases.

Hazard Communication Guidelines. While on the job, every person has a right to be protected from obvious hazards and illness. However, building companies and their superintendents are also now faced with the task of informing their workers regarding certain job-related hazards that may not be quite so obvious. OSHA currently has full and immediate authority to conduct HazCom inspections of all construction companies and jobsites. Citations and possible fines of up to $10,000 per violation have been issued for noncompliance.

All building companies and contractors, no matter how large or small, are required to comply with the OSHA HazCom Standard. Employers must inform and train their employees about all hazardous substances they are working with, as well as those materials they might come into contact with from other trades.

There are four main elements of HazCom compliance:

- preparing a written hazard communication program for your company
- labeling products and containers
- providing Material Safety Data Sheets (MSDSs)
- training employees

The National Association of Home Builders, Associated Builders and Contractors, and the American Subcontractors Association have developed a comprehensive, step-by-step compliance kit that has been praised by OSHA. This Hazard Communication Kit is available from NAHB, and many additional materials about safety and health are available through NAHB's Labor, Safety, and Health Services department.

Chapter 3

Quality Control and Inspections

Introduction

Of the superintendent's three primary responsibilities, quality control will have the greatest impact on overall long-term success. Your reputation as a builder and your future success will depend greatly on the quality of your work. Most builders depend heavily on referrals for future business, and referrals come from quality work. Quality control on the construction site is based on three basic responsibilities:

- establishing the performance standards required for both materials and workmanship
- establishing procedures to ensure that these standards are met
- judging whether or not completed work meets the established standards

When determining the level of quality required, you are obligated to follow the dictates of those to whom you report. As a matter of policy, the builder, in cooperation with subs, suppliers, and in-house employees, will ordinarily establish standards mutually acceptable to both the company and to the homeowner. It then becomes your responsibility to determine whether or not the work meets these standards.

The best superintendents learn to judge work quality through years of valuable experience. However, less experienced superintendents can upgrade their skills in various ways:

- talking with experienced superintendents and asking questions
- reading books and articles on quality management
- using educational audiotapes and videotapes
- talking with municipal inspectors

A wealth of information on quality is available. The current excitement surrounding the Total Quality Management movement has been the inspiration for numerous books and articles. NAHB has a number of current publications on the subject. In addition, *Professional Builder*, *Builder*, and other trade publications frequently have excellent articles on quality management.

Responsibility for Quality Control

You should keep in mind that quality control is not the superintendent's exclusive domain, but requires the participation of everyone involved in the construction process: architects, homeowners, contractors, salespeople, superintendents, suppliers, inspectors, lending institutions, and especially laborers and subcontractors. All members of the building team have a responsibility to ensure that their work meets the mutually accepted standards and that the materials used are of a quality equal to or better than the materials specified.

Creating an Atmosphere of High Quality

The best insurance of a high-quality job is a two-step process. First, you must establish internally what the levels of performance and standards for quality will be. Second, you must communicate these standards to customers and set their level of expectation. Larger builders use model homes to demonstrate their quality, style, and craftsmanship. Smaller builders can use other means, such as mockups, photos, and other demonstrations.

Attitudes have a direct impact on the quality of construction work. Every worker possesses an innate desire to produce high-quality work, and you should make every effort to cultivate this attitude and motivate the worker. A company that emphasizes high quality inspires excellent workmanship.

As an example, one company has implemented a program called PRIDE: Personal Responsibility in Daily Excellence. PRIDE is aimed at motivating individual workers to peak performance. It lets employees know how important they are and helps them develop new confidence and self-esteem. By taking responsibility for their own work, employees satisfy their own needs for recognition. In addition, employees responsible for improved quality are given sizable monetary rewards.

Performance Standards

Performance standards are the basis of any quality control system and should be in writing. These standards communicate to those involved what is to be built, the criteria to be used in judging quality, and the specifications required. Management should devote the time necessary to make certain that all standards are precise, understandable, and based on measurable criteria. Once standards are set, they must be communicated to those responsible for carrying them out. You might find it beneficial to provide employees and subcontractors with a copy of the standards that apply to them. Consider taking a creative approach to quality management. Have an annual or semiannual breakfast meeting with subs to re-emphasize standards and mutual benefits of quality. Call it a "subcontractor appreciation breakfast."

Training

Training in-house is generally a good idea for large and small firms. However, subcontractors and material suppliers can also be trained, resulting in better quality control. This type of training can usually be accomplished through onsite inspections with subs, in-house sessions and informal discussions, or through seminars sponsored by NAHB and other organizations.

Informal inspections and critique sessions conducted by experienced quality control inspectors can also serve as an excellent teaching aid.

Inspections

If all work is inspected and approved as the project progresses, fewer problems will develop at inspection time. This emphasis on quality control should begin with the builder and trickle down through the entire company structure. Without the active support of upper management, mottos, slogans, and signs are simply wasted effort.

Internal Inspections

Internal inspections must be timely if they are to be of any value. As the superintendent responsible for quality control, you should actively inspect each project daily, even if projects are on widely scattered lots. These checks should verify whether work is progressing as scheduled. They also allow the superintendent to inspect work completed since the last visit.

Builders without formal quality control systems often rely heavily on public inspectors to detect faults, provide punch lists, or identify corrections. This practice is risky and unnecessary. Each company should conduct its own internal inspections if it wants to reduce the risk of inferior work and expensive rework.

Inspection Checklists

When conducting their own inspections, many superintendents use inspection checklists tailored to their particular organization (see Figures 3.1 to 3.10, beginning on page 34). These checklists serve as memory joggers, prompting you to look for crucial items. Inspection checklists should include information on any items that:

- have been problems in the past
- are difficult to repair or replace if they are covered up
- are particularly important to quality in the eyes of the customer

Quality control checklists are invaluable tools for monitoring the quality and completeness of work. They can help ensure that minimum standards of quality are met. The quality control checklists in Figures 3.1 through 3.10 cover key stages in the construction process. However, checklists can be developed and adapted for many production steps, including:

- excavation quality
- footer quality
- foundation inspection
- backfilling inspection
- exterior concrete flatwork quality
- interior concrete flatwork quality
- framing quality
- finish carpentry quality
- HVAC rough quality
- plumbing rough quality
- electrical rough quality
- roofing quality
- brick quality
- insulation quality
- drywall quality
- electrical finish quality
- plumbing finish quality
- HVAC finish quality
- pre walk-through

Your company should carefully adapt all quality control checklists to include specific standards that are both measurable and attainable.

Preinspections

Inspections required by local building codes, FHA/VA, and lending institutions are usually intended only to ensure compliance with standards of safety and structural integrity, rather than to deal specifically with quality control. Nonetheless, you should conduct preinspection checks in order to detect and correct any problems before the inspector arrives. This worthwhile practice can serve to:

- prevent rejection by the inspector
- eliminate the cost of reinspection fees
- maintain your company's reputation as a high-quality builder

Gaining Cooperation

During outside inspections, you may find it best to develop a cooperative attitude, extending courtesy toward inspectors whenever possible.

Inspectors tend to be more cooperative under such circumstances. To develop this atmosphere of cooperation, you should follow these guidelines:

- Know the applicable building codes inside and out.
- Know what additional permit requirements have been established through the legal process by the local building department.
- Know what things inspectors would like to see but which are not official policies or standards.
- Schedule inspections following the procedures of the inspection department, and as far in advance as possible.
- Have subcontractors check their work to make sure it is ready.
- Check the job yourself to make sure that it is ready before calling for an inspection.
- If a job is not ready when an inspection is scheduled, notify the inspector as soon as you are aware of a delay.
- Be available to the inspector during the inspection whenever possible.
- Keep in mind that the inspector's interpretation of the codes can be as important as the letter of the code.
- Cooperate with the inspectors by promptly correcting work that is below standard.
- If the inspector requires something above and beyond the code requirement, find out why, and if the reasoning is sound, comply with the request.

Making yourself available is the most important key to passing your inspections the first time. If you are on the job when the inspector comes, you can correct most of the items immediately while the inspector is there. Once you have gained their confidence, more often than not, inspectors will take your word that you will correct many of the other items and allow you to continue without a reinspection. Don't be defensive. If the inspector takes your word that an item will be corrected, make sure it is. The first time you fail to keep your word will be the last time you will have the opportunity. If the inspector asks you to do something for which compliance seems unreasonable, try negotiating first. Refusing to comply may create hard feelings and can lead to considerable delays while both parties attempt to prove their points. Cooperation is always better than alienation.

If you experience a persistent problem with getting something to pass inspection and you feel you are correct in the way that you do something, work directly with the chief building official to get it resolved. If that doesn't work, get together with other builders in your local BIA or HBA and flex some combined muscle to get the policy or requirement changed.

Making Corrections

All construction team members have the ultimate responsibility of ensuring that their work is equal to or better than the quality specified. However, the superintendent is in the best position to enforce these standards. Performance should be judged on the basis of compliance with the standards, and the individual or firm who completed the work should be responsible for any necessary corrective action. One of the keys to good customer relations is to respond to any concerns customers might have, even though it might not be important to you in terms of the overall construction process. It is imperative that you promptly correct anything that the customer notices to be of substandard quality. If you delay correcting these things until later, the procrastination may cause the customer to feel uneasy and may strain the relationship you have built.

Inspection Points

The following inspection points are critical:

- prior to placing concrete footings and foundations
- prior to placing concrete floors
- on the final day of rough framing (while the framer is still finishing up)
- upon completion of rough mechanical work
- after rough electrical and plumbing
- when wall insulation is being installed
- when drywall is up and taped (prior to painting)
- upon project completion
- others as required by the local building department

Each of these inspections should be considered mandatory, and each is required by most building inspection departments.

Logging Inspections

All required inspections should be noted on the construction schedule and recorded in the daily log book. The daily log should contain records of both in-house and outside inspections, including the following:

- date and time of the inspection
- name of the inspector
- nature of the inspection
- results of the inspection
- notes on any special circumstances
- inspector's signature, where applicable

Be sure to keep good track of the inspection card. It is your only legal proof that an inspection has passed. During inspections, it is usually required to be posted on the jobsite. However, you may want to consider keeping it in a more secure place between inspections.

Final Inspection

The final inspection before the customer walk-through and orientation is one of the most important. Conduct your own personal inspection first. Make sure you are satisfied that the job is complete. You may want to have your immediate supervisor or another superintendent conduct this inspection and be very critical of even small discrepancies. This inspection serves as a check and balance procedure for the superintendent, whose familiarity with the job day after day may cause him or her to miss small flaws. Being supercritical at this point will cut down on customer complaints and enhance the builder's reputation for quality.

Customer Walk-Through and Orientation

If the proper inspections have already taken place, the customer walk-through and orientation can be a positive, rewarding experience, rather than something to be dreaded by everyone involved. Some builders even invite subcontractors to be present in order to demonstrate the operation and maintenance of their products. Subcontractors installing complex systems, such as lawn sprinklers or security systems, are particularly well suited to this approach. They can also explain any warranties involved and discuss how customer service requests will be handled. Their presence helps to make customers aware of their own responsibilities for maintenance and establishes a means of satisfaction for many customer complaints. Instead of simply having the customer look for flaws or imperfections, accentuate the positive aspects of the home. For further information on the customer walk-through and orientation, see Chapter 7, Working with the Buyer.

Figure 3.1 Footer Quality Checklist

Job number: _____   Date: _____

❏ Inspection completed and inspection card signed.

❏ Correct front yard set back ± 1 in. _____ ft.

❏ Parallel to the street (where applicable) ± 1 in.

❏ Correct side yard set backs ± 1 in. _____ ft. left side, _____ ft. right side.

❏ Rear yard set back ± 1 in. _____ ft.

❏ Check for presence of groundwater or soft spots in the soil before forming the footings.

❏ Footer depth will be below the frost line (36 in. in most areas).

❏ Check for proper elevation. Backfill should provide for 6 in. in 10 ft. of fall away from the house.

❏ Soil under footer is undisturbed.

❏ Footer steps properly formed.

❏ Forms properly staked and nailed.

❏ Check *all* dimensions.

❏ Standard footer depth is ___ in. ± 1 in. Width is ___ in. ± 1 in. Footer should extend 4-5 in. on each side of the block foundation wall.

❏ The length is correct, all sides, to within +½ in. (*but not short!*)

❏ Diagonal measurements equal ± ½ in.

❏ Check location and dimensions of offsets and jobs for fireplaces stoops, porches, etc.

❏ Check location and size of post pads and piers.

❏ Forms level ± ¼ in. 10 ft. and ± ½ in. overall.

❏ Bulkheads correct size and location.

❏ Blockouts provided for utilities and located ± 3 in. of specified.

❏ Check location of bleeders and sump pump.

❏ Footer concrete _____ bag mix or _____ psi.

❏ Maximum slump 5 in. ± 1 in.

❏ If at all possible the pour should be one continuous pour.

❏ The concrete is poured as nearly as possible to final position.

❏ It is finished flat & level ± ¼ in. in 10 ft., not more than ½ in. overall, and left rough.

❏ All bulkhead forms are stripped and removed following proper curing time and not less than 12 hours, depending on temperature.

❏ Drain tile installed properly and covered with gravel.

❏ Site cleaned up after subcontractor is finished; any waste material is stored in the designated location.

❏ Proper steps taken to keep concrete from freezing in cold weather or drying too fast in hot weather or high winds.

❏ Soil unfrozen, without snow or ice.

❏ Footers covered with 24 in. to 36 in. of straw or other insulation depending on temperature.

Signature: _____

The measurements given represent standards used by one construction company; they may not be suited to all construction companies in all regions. Consult your local building codes and individual company standards before adapting and using this checklist.

Figure 3.2 Foundation Inspection Sheet

Job number: _____   Date: _____

❑ Inspection completed and inspection card signed.

❑ Location. Recheck proper setbacks and alignment.

❑ Check block thickness of foundation ___ in.

❑ The concrete foundation should be centered on the footer. There should be at least 4 in. of concrete footer on each side of the foundation.

❑ Check *all* dimensions according to the following tolerances.

Overall length	± ¼ in.
Overall width	± ¼ in.
Diagonal measurement	± ½ in.
Plumb	± ¼ in. in 8 ft.
Level	± ¼ in.

❑ Walls square ± ¼ in. in 20 ft. Not more than ½ in. out of square in any dimension.

❑ Walls straight ± ¼ in. in 20 ft. Not more than ± ½ in. overall in any wall.

❑ Offsets for fireplaces, stairways, etc.: Location ± ¼ in., size ± ¼ in.

❑ Windows & doors located as specified.

❑ Windows & doors placed level ± ⅛ in.

❑ Windows & doors openings sized *not smaller* and to within ¼ in. in all dimensions.

❑ Basement walkouts correct size and location.

❑ Windows ¼ in. below top of wall and grouted into plumb position.

❑ Brick ledge correct location and size.

❑ Beam pockets correct height, size, and location ± ¼ in. and reinforced with #4 rebar.

❑ Garage returns and center piers correct size and location.

❑ Block ledge extended out to support garage slab, stoops, and porches per print.

❑ Foundation bolts or hold down anchor straps are placed 6 ft. o.c. Bolts or straps are placed within 12 in. of each corner in both directions.

❑ J-bolts or anchors centered in sill plate.

❑ All bolts are placed in concrete grout, *not mortar,* 15 in. min. straps

❑ Post pads in proper location— 24 in. x 24 in. x 12 in. —1 in. lower than footings

❑ Seam between foundation and footer sealed watertight.

❑ Damp proofing, good complete coverage, no missed spots.

❑ Parging is ⅜-in. thick and covered at the bottom of the wall where it meets the footing.

❑ All joints on block walls tooled both inside and outside, above and below grade.

❑ Cores on block walls poured with concrete grout *not mortar* according to the prints or drawings.

❑ Confirm that ½ in. rebar is in each poured core.

❑ Corners should be weaved together. Stack bond or cold joints should not be used.

❑ Intersecting walls tied in properly at 5th and 8th courses with Durawall or other reinforcement.

❑ Block walls braced properly prior to backfill.

❑ Excess mortar cleaned off the foundation and the footer.

❑ Site is cleaned up after mason is finished.

Signature: _____

The measurements given represent standards used by one construction company; they may not be suited to all construction companies in all regions. Consult your local building codes and individual company standards before adapting and using this checklist.

Figure 3.3 Backfilling Quality Checklist

Job number: _____   Date: _____

❑ Foundation damp proofing complete according to quality standards.

❑ Footer drains properly installed.

❑ Gravel in place around footer tile to proper depth.

❑ All debris and garbage removed from trenches.

❑ Check sump crocks for location and elevation.

❑ Utility lines installed as required.

❑ Foundation is properly braced.

❑ Pile of dirt used for backfilling is free of debris, large rocks, and other material that could damage the foundation wall and footing tile.

❑ Material placed in 18-in. to 24-in. lifts. No large rocks, boulders, or clumps of clay were allowed to fall against or damage the foundation walls and footing tile.

❑ Rough grade provides a minimum of 10 in. of fall away from the foundation for a distance of at least 20 ft.

❑ If necessary provide swales to divert water away from foundation.

Signature: _____

The measurements given represent standards used by one construction company; they may not be suited to all construction companies in all regions. Consult your local building codes and individual company standards before adapting and using this checklist.

Figure 3.4 Framing Quality Checklist

Job number: _____   Date: _____

❑ All lumber meets or exceeds CABO code requirements and spec. requirements.

❑ All lumber in contact with concrete or soil is pressure treated wood.

Floors

❑ Sill sealer insulation installed between foundation sill plates and concrete.

❑ Sill plate fastened with foundation bolts or anchor straps every 6 ft. o.c.

❑ Washers and nuts securely in place.

❑ Bolts or anchor straps are located within 12 in. of the corner in both directions and located within 16 in. of the end of each plate. Power-actuated fasteners located every 16 in. o.c. where bolts are missing.

❑ Foundation plates square ± ¼ in. in 10 ft. Diagonal measurements are equal ± ½ in.

❑ Nail wood basement windows to the mud sill in a plumb position.

❑ Jack post placed directly over post footings, centered on the beam, and plumb within ¼ in.

❑ Beam nailed according to CABO code and specs.

❑ Minimum head clearance 6 ft. 4 in. between bottom of beams and floor.

❑ Spliced-in built-up beams occur over adjustable posts or per engineered specs.

❑ Jack post nailed to beam.

❑ Floor joists are of grade and species of lumber as specified.

❑ Joists 16 inches o.c. unless indicated otherwise in specs.

❑ Floor joists properly spaced to allow for the pass-through of plumbing, heating and air-conditioning ducts, and electric equipment as required by plans and specifications.

❑ Minimum bearing of floor joists is 1½ in.

❑ Where styrofoam or high R-value sheathing is used on exterior walls, rim joists and header joists are held in the thickness of the sheathing.

❑ Rim joist toe-nailed to mud sill plate every 16 in. with 16d nails.

❑ Rim joist straight ± ¼.

❑ Joists and beams are checked to make sure that they are according to the proper size and span for the particular species and grade of lumber used.

❑ Floor joists crowned up.

❑ Level within ± ¼ in.

❑ Each joist is nailed to the rim joist with at least three 16d nails.

❑ Floor joists are toe-nailed with two 10d box nails to center bearing partitions or girders.

❑ Floor joists which are doubled are nailed together with 12d nails at 16 in. o.c.

❑ The last joist of layout is spaced to allow proper insulation.

❑ Double floor joists installed around stairwell openings, at bearing walls, and at other locations as required by the plans and specifications.

❑ Add a 2x10 to rim joists over basement windows.

❑ Add double 2x10 blocking under jack studs at patio doors over 6 ft. rough openings.

❑ Joist hangers installed and nailed where no solid bearing is provided.

❑ Notches, holes, or cuts, if necessary, are made in the center of joists' width, not on the top or bottom edges.

❑ Notches, holes, or cuts, if necessary, are made in the first third of the joist span, not on the center ⅓ of the span.

❑ Check the span of the joist using the CABO Span Tables.

❑ Bridging installed and nailed.

(continued)

Figure 3.4 Framing Quality Checklist (continued)

❏ Construction adhesive used under all floor sheathing.

❏ Plywood or OSB subfloor nailed 6 in. o.c. on edges, 12 in. o.c. at intermediate supports.

❏ 1/16 in. to ⅛ in. spacing around plywood or OSB sheets for expansion or T&G sheets used.

❏ 2 in. dead air space around all masonry fire-places.

❏ Stairwell is located correctly ± 1 in.

❏ Check stair risers to see if all are equal ± ⅛ in. and between 7 and 8 inches.

❏ Check treads for level.

❏ Check stair horses for cracks.

❏ Minimum head room 6 ft. 8 in. at all stairways.

Walls

❏ Plywood/OSB or T-bracing at corners and every 25 ft. according to prints. Nailed with 10d nails at top and bottom plates and 10d nails for each stud.

❏ Studs laid out at 16 in. o.c.

❏ Stud layout started at the same end as the floor joist layout.

❏ Three-stud corners.

❏ Crown all studs the same way.

❏ Check for bowed studs.

❏ Two 16d nails per stud, both ends.

❏ Anchor bolts on garage walls are placed as close to the middle of the plate as possible and at intervals of every 6 ft. o.c.

❏ House dimensions are as specified ± ¼ in. (perimeter).

❏ Wall plumb ± ¼ in. in 8 ft.

❏ Bottom plate nailed to floor 16 in. o.c.

❏ Splices in plates occur over studs.

❏ All splices in the double top plate occur at least 4 ft. from a splice in the top plate.

❏ All exterior wall intersections are insulatable.

❏ Trimmer stud and header joints tight.

❏ All walls, studs, headers, plates nailed securely per code.

❏ Headers meet code requirements for span.

❏ Garage door headers properly built and crowned up.

❏ Garage door trimmer studs have 2x6 jambs and brick mold installed. Counter 2x4 casing on the inside. Center of garage door has a spring block.

❏ Trimmer stud and header joints tight.

❏ All walls, studs, headers, plates nailed securely per CABO code requirements.

❏ Garage door jambs and brick mold installed.

❏ All warped studs removed or straightened. Warped studs in interior walls cut straight and full-length scabs placed on each side of the cut. Warped studs in exterior walls or load-bearing walls are removed and replaced or cut straight and doubled up.

❏ Styrofoam and fiberboard sheathing installed with tight joints and nailed 3 in. o.c. on edges and 6 in. o.c. in the field. Plywood and OSB 6 in. o.c. in the field.

❏ 2 in. dead air space around all masonry fire-places.

❏ Check walls around cabinets to make sure that they are straight and there are no studs that are abnormally curved and that the corners are square, so that when the cabinets are installed they will line up with the walls properly.

❏ Draft stops are installed at the drop ceiling or cabinet drop as required.

❏ Bearing wall studs are not notched more than 25% of the width of the studs, non bearing wall studs are not notched more than 40% of the width of the studs.

❏ Holes drilled in studs do not exceed more than 40% of the stud width and are at least ⅝ in. from the edge of the stud.

❏ Backing installed for any interior or exterior hand rails.

(continued)

Figure 3.4 Framing Quality Checklist (continued)

❏ Draft stops installed wherever required by code (stairs, 10-ft. walls, etc.).

❏ Backing installed for cabinets, grab bars, etc.

Interior Partitions

❏ Studs crowned the same way.

❏ Studs spaced evenly 16 o.c. unless specified otherwise.

❏ Walls located ± ½ in. as per plans.

❏ Plumb ± ¼ in. in 8 ft.

❏ Bath tub opening _____ in.

❏ Insulation installed properly behind the tub.

❏ One-piece tubs installed correctly.

❏ Check shower stall measurements.

❏ Check vanity depth to make sure casing won't hit vanity top.

❏ Hallways 37 in. rough width unless otherwise specified.

❏ Half walls securely anchored by extending end studs through the floor and anchoring them to the floor joists.

❏ Closets 25 in. deep unless otherwise specified.

❏ Walls which contain bathroom chases or bathroom plumbing pipes are of sufficient size to contain the pipes that will be placed therein.

❏ Headers over interior partitions and non load-bearing partitions are constructed without built-up headers since there is no load placed on them.

❏ Bottom plates are nailed to the floor 16 in. o.c.

❏ All walls in place as per plans.

❏ Top plate should be tight against bottom truss cord.

❏ All medicine cabinets framed per print unless otherwise specified.

❏ All warped studs removed or straightened. Warped studs in interior walls replaced or cut straight and full-length scabs placed on each side of the cut. Warped studs in exterior walls or load bearing walls are removed and replaced or cut straightened and doubled up.

❏ All drywall backing is installed.

❏ Backing for cabinets, grab bars, etc.

Windows and Doors

❏ Mark door swings on the floor with crayon or paint.

❏ Door openings plumb ± ¼ in.

❏ Entry doors are raised up by adding a ¾ ft. board to the bottom of the threshold. The ¾ in. board is caulked to the threshold on the top and glued to the floor on the bottom.

❏ Doors properly shimmed, especially at each hinge and at the strike plate.

❏ Exterior doors _____ in. high, 2 in. wider than door.

❏ Swinging doors _____ in. high, 2 in. wider than door.

❏ Bypass doors _____ in. high, 1 in. less than the width of both doors (48 in. = 47 in., 60 in. = 59 in., etc.).

❏ Bifold doors _____ in. high, 1½ in. wider than doors.

❏ All trimmer and king studs and headers around bypass and bifold door openings must be perfectly plumb, straight, and level. Use the best clear and straight lumber for these areas.

❏ Openings located as specified ± 1 in.

❏ Exterior door shimmed and securely installed and nailed in at least four places on each jamb and the long screws are in place in the top hinge.

❏ Exterior doors are plumb and operate correctly.

❏ A 2-in. CCA kick plate should be placed on the outside of the house to support the threshold on exterior doors.

❏ Patio doors are properly shimmed installed with three screws in the header.

(continued)

Figure 3.4 Framing Quality Checklist (continued)

❏ Check kitchen window width to assure window is located according to plans and according to the cabinet layout ± ¼ in.

❏ Windows openings framed as specified ± ¼ in. per manufacturer's specs.

❏ Patio doors framed per rough openings on print.

❏ Sliding glass framed as specified ± ¼ in.

❏ Windows installed level, plumb, and square ± ⅛ in.

❏ Windows properly shimmed and nailed at 16 in. o.c. or per manufacturer's specs.

❏ Twin and triple windows are shimmed between the sill and where the windows join for adequate support.

❏ Window sill height as specified ± ¼ in. (especially in the kitchen).

❏ Interior non-load-bearing wall headers are built with blocking, not solid lumber.

❏ Check to assure window is not in upside down or backwards.

❏ Bay windows properly insulated.

❏ All windows and doors operate and seal properly.

Roof Framing

❏ Trusses erected according to plan.

❏ Trusses fit properly on the wall—the bearing points are correct.

❏ Trusses toe-nailed to top plates with two 10d nails.

❏ Check cantilever trusses.

❏ Truss anchors installed on both ends of every truss.

❏ Trusses fastened to top plate of the center wall with truss anchors. Truss anchors are staggered on each side of the top plate.

❏ Truss anchors installed correctly.

❏ 1x4 catwalk installed 8 ft. o.c. where there is no center wall to help stabilize trusses.

❏ 2x4 crow's-foot wind brace installed at gable ends.

❏ Attic vents installed properly.

❏ Trusses uncut, cracked, or broken anywhere. If trusses get broken contact truss manufacturer to determine most effective correction measures.

❏ Header properly installed to take the load on recessed entries, windows, and doorways.

❏ Rafters are checked to ensure proper sizing, spacing, and species of lumber.

❏ A minimum bearing surface of 3 in. is required of all rafters.

❏ Bridging is installed where necessary.

❏ Lateral bracing installed per truss specs.

❏ All bird's-mouth and other cuts are checked to make sure that excess material has not been cut away and that they align properly.

❏ All collar beams and other beam material is of the proper species, size, and spacing.

❏ Soffit nailers at porches installed correctly.

❏ Gable end blocking installed at peak at every 8 ft. in soffit if plywood soffit is used on gable ends.

❏ Roof sheathing nailed 8 in. o.c. on edges and 12 in. o.c. at supports.

❏ Ply clips installed in all roof sheathing.

❏ Stand back and check the roof from a substantial distance in a number of different directions and check the roof to see if it looks right. Is the fascia straight and plumb and level? Are the walls on the outside structure straight? Does the building simply look right?

❏ False fascia and fly rafters installed straight and securely.

❏ Standard gable overhang is 11 in. Check print to confirm.

❏ Fly rafters properly blocked according to prints.

❏ Attic access properly framed and designed for drywaller 22 in. x 32 in. inside the house 22 in. x 48 in. in finished garages.

❏ Double studs under girder truss bearing points or as specified.

(continued)

Figure 3.4 Framing Quality Checklist (continued)

❏ Joist hangers installed on girder trusses.

❏ Cricket or saddle installed behind all chimneys to divert water, snow, and ice.

❏ Felt paper and drip edge installed as soon as sheathing is properly nailed and fly rafters are installed.

Backing

❏ Backing for cabinets installed.

❏ Backing for grab bars, towel bars, etc.

❏ Backing for closet shelves.

❏ Cabinet soffits are the correct size and straight, plumb and level. (Check carefully with a tape, square and level).

❏ Check stairs for turned posts and railing.

❏ Fire blocking installed at cabinet drops.

❏ Fire blocking installed wherever required by local code.

Miscellaneous

❏ Skylights properly framed and flashed.

❏ Dimensions for cabinet drops checked and re-checked.

❏ Fire blocking installed at cabinet drops.

❏ Cross supports in porch ceiling to support soffit, level with fascia.

❏ Porch post installed in proper location inside the foundation block and plumb within $\frac{1}{4}$ in.

❏ Cantilevered porches have a 2x4 nailer placed vertically where the post will be eventually located so the siding crew can install siding around the post.

❏ Stairs meet code requirements for maximum rise (8 in.) and minimum run (9 in.).

❏ All stair rises are equal ± $\frac{1}{8}$ in.

❏ Stair treads are level.

❏ Dropped ceiling installed in stairwells.

❏ All split levels have $\frac{1}{2}$ in. CDX plywood or OSB installed on utility/basement wall.

❏ Change orders have been checked to verify that no changes have been made to sheetrock.

Overall Framing Inspection

❏ Stand back and look at the building at a distance to see if all appears centered, leveled and straight.

❏ All windows are located properly as per the elevations.

❏ All exterior doors are installed and temporary locks are installed to secure the building.

❏ Exterior door swing properly and are sealed tightly.

❏ Check floors for squeaks.

❏ All trash and debris have been cleaned up from throughout the site.

❏ The house was swept and left broom-clean by the framer.

❏ Extra material is returned for credit.

Signature: _____

The measurements given represent standards used by one construction company; they may not be suited to all construction companies in all regions. Consult your local building codes and individual company standards before adapting and using this checklist.

Figure 3.5 Insulation Quality Checklist

Job number: _____   Date: _____

❑ Gaps around windows foam-insulated or caulked on the sides and top. Stuffed with batt insulation on the sills.

❑ Gaps around exterior doors foam insulated or caulked.

❑ Rim joists, vertical joints at outside corners, and bottom plates on exterior or garage walls sealed and caulked.

❑ All pipes and outlets boxes penetrating outside walls sealed or insulated.

❑ Cracks or holes in exterior sheathing sealed with foam prior to batts being installed.

❑ All chase openings or kitchen drops sealed.

❑ Header or rim joists insulated properly.

❑ R-Values as specified. Unless specified otherwise:

Exterior walls	R-___	Friction fit
Cantilever areas	R-___	Craft-faced insulation
Furred block walls	R-___	Friction fit
Basements (optional)	R-___	Foil-faced insulation 48 in. wide
Rim joists	R-___	Friction fit
Crawl space (electric heat)	R-___	Foil-faced insulation 48 in. wide
Ceiling	R-___	Blown insulation

❑ All holes penetrating double top plate are sealed.

❑ Exterior insulative sheathing from top plate to bottom of mudsill.

❑ Exterior sheathing butts up tightly.

❑ Exterior sheathing holes repaired and taped properly.

❑ Wall insulation batts not compressed.

❑ Tightly cut to fit irregular spaces.

❑ Snug fit on studs/plates.

❑ Behind tubs, vents and chimneys.

❑ No insulation within 1½ in. of B-vents. Unfaced insulation only near B-vents.

❑ Split insulation batts for pipes and electrical wires in exterior walls.

❑ Cut out for electrical boxes, no compression insulation cutout placed behind the electrical box.

❑ Vapor barrier, 2 mil. polyethylene, installed properly, no holes, splices overlap, proper thickness, etc.

❑ Corners and small holes insulated properly.

❑ Insulation baffles between rafters and trusses installed properly.

❑ Insulation depth gauge sticks are provided in all blown-in insulation areas.

❑ Ceilings properly insulated.

❑ Insulation collar installed around attic access.

❑ Insulation gauge strips installed.

❑ Certificate of compliance filled out and nailed to trusses near attic access.

❑ Statement of R-Value stapled to side of attic access opening.

❑ Access hatch insulated to the same R-Value as the rest of the ceiling.

❑ Soffit spaces over top plates and up to the insulation baffles fully insulated.

❑ Cantilever spaces fully insulated.

❑ Miscellaneous spaces filled and insulated.

❑ The house was swept including in between studs and left broom-clean by the insulator.

❑ Scrap material was placed in the trash pile.

Signature: _____

The measurements given represent standards used by one construction company; they may not be suited to all construction companies in all regions. Consult your local building codes and individual company standards before adapting and using this checklist.

Figure 3.6 Interior Concrete Flatwork Quality Checklist

Job number: _____   Date: _____

❏ All plumbing installed, inspected, and approved.

❏ All plumbing has been tested.

❏ Floor drains shall be installed so water will drain into floor drain in prescribed area with a slope of $\frac{1}{8}$ in. to $\frac{1}{4}$ in. per foot.

❏ Sump wells are in place and bleeders are tied in.

❏ Garages with basement doorways have a fume barrier.

❏ Underground ducts and mechanical chases are in (if applicable).

❏ 4 in. of gravel is in place and level 1 in.

❏ Vapor barrier is in place if required.

❏ Concrete slab reinforced as per code and according to plans and specs.

❏ Concrete slab 3 in. thick unless specified otherwise.

❏ If welded wire mesh is used, it is brought up off the ground at least $1\frac{1}{2}$ in.

❏ Absolutely no aluminum to be embedded in the concrete!

❏ A parting agent has been sprayed on the concrete foundation and footers prior to placing the floor so the floor does not adhere to them.

❏ Floor concrete _____ bag mix or _____ psi.

❏ Max slump 5 in. 1 in.

❏ Air entrainment 6% ± 1%.

❏ Do not sprinkle water on surface to make troweling easier.

❏ If at all possible, the pour should be one continuous pour.

❏ The concrete is deposited as nearly as possible to final position.

❏ Level of ± $\frac{1}{4}$ in. in 10 ft. and 1 in. overall.

❏ All concrete has expansion joints placed approximately 10 ft. o.c.

❏ The individual pads created by the expansion joints form a square (equal sides) as much as possible.

❏ Avoid premature finishing while bleed water is present.

❏ Any forms are stripped and removed after no less than 12 hours, depending on temperature. Care should be taken so as not to damage fresh concrete.

❏ Concrete sprayed with curing compound as soon as possible following finishing. Coverage should be complete and of sufficient thickness to ensure adequate curing.

❏ Maintain concrete above 50° F. for 3 days.

❏ Jobsite clean up of all excess concrete and form material.

❏ Area is free from snow, ice, and debris.

❏ Proper steps taken to keep concrete from freezing in cold weather or drying too fast in hot weather.

❏ Slabs are covered with 24 in. to 36 in. of straw or other insulation, depending on temperature or heated if temperature is below 32°F at night.

Signature: _____

The measurements given represent standards used by one construction company; they may not be suited to all construction companies in all regions. Consult your local building codes and individual company standards before adapting and using this checklist.

Figure 3.7 Plumbing Rough Quality Checklist

Job number: _____   Date: _____

Plumbing First Rough Below Grade or Slab

❑ Check correct location and layout of all fixtures and drains per blueprint and verify.

❑ Make sure all drainage pipes are sloped ⅛ in. per foot.

❑ Any overexcavated trenches are properly compacted prior to installing the pipe.

❑ Check cleanout locations (typically required every 50 ft.).

❑ Box out trap areas.

❑ Check water line location; make sure it is correct.

❑ All drainage pipes tested with 10 in. head of water for 15 minutes or 5 psi of air for 15 minutes.

❑ Must hand-backfill this area.

❑ Inspection card is filled out and signed prior to pour.

House Plumbing Rough-In

❑ No plumbing is run in exterior walls.

❑ Make sure that all water and drainage lines are properly supported.

❑ Make sure the cleanout is accessible.

❑ Make sure vent lines at roof are properly flashed with a roof jack.

❑ Make sure copper lines are neat and go where they are supposed to go and are properly supported to avoid squeaks.

❑ Make sure tub is properly installed and nail flange is nailed with 8d nails 16 in. o.c.

❑ Check for any tub damage.

❑ Studs in an exterior or bearing wall should not be notched more than 25% of their width. 2x4 = 1 in., 2x6 = 1¼. Studs on interior or nonbearing walls should not be notched more than 40% of their width. 2x4 = 1⅝, 2x6 = 2 in.

❑ Studs may be drilled a maximum of 40% of their width provided the hole is no closer than ⅝ in. from edge of the stud and the stud is not notched.

❑ Holes in floor joists should not be more than ⅓ of the depth of the joist in diameter and should not be located within 2 in. of the top or bottom of the joist.

❑ Notches in the joists should not exceed 1/6 of the depth of the joist and should not be located within the middle of the third span.

❑ Roof trusses should not be drilled, cut, or notched.

❑ Plumbing lines not too close to the edge of the wall.

❑ Steel protection plates are used whenever plumbing pipes are closer than 1½ in. from the edge of the plate or stud.

❑ Confirm the location of each plumbing fixture using the print.

❑ No more than three fixtures can be supplied by a ½-in. supply line.

❑ Jetted tubs with pumps must have access to the pumps.

❑ All drainage pipes tested with 10 in. head of water for 15 minutes or 5 psi of air for 15 minutes.

❑ All supply pipes were tested with 150 psi for 15 minutes.

❑ Seal all air conditioning lines that exit the house with rope caulk.

❑ Toilets are at least 12 in. from the finished wall surface.

❑ Convert plastic piping to copper at shower heads and faucets and secure properly.

❑ Cover tubs with cardboard or plastic to protect them.

(continued)

Figure 3.7 Plumbing Rough Quality Checklist (continued)

❏ Tubs and showers on exterior walls are insulated behind them prior to being set.

❏ Make sure soil pipe exit is sealed and completely tarred.

❏ Frost-proof faucets installed.

❏ Check locations for future decks, porches and steps.

❏ Test caps removed on vent stacks.

❏ Roof jacks (plumbing vent collars) are installed.

❏ Inspection card is filled out and signed.

❏ House is swept and left broom-clean by the plumber.

Signature: _____

The measurements given represent standards used by one construction company; they may not be suited to all construction companies in all regions. Consult your local building codes and individual company standards before adapting and using this checklist.

Figure 3.8 Roofing Quality Checklist

Job number: _____   Date: _____

❏ Felt paper checked for tears and missing paper and properly repaired before shingles are installed.

❏ Shingles are the correct color as specified by the owner (check the color section chart).

❏ Shingles overhang the eaves and drip edge by _____ in. and the gable ends by ½ in.

❏ Shingle exposure is _____ in. maximum.

❏ Shingles are installed horizontally so that there are no noticeable color differences from one bundle to another.

❏ Shingles are laid straight and line up horizontally and vertically according to manufacturer's instructions.

❏ Roof jacks (roof vent collars) caulked or sealed with black plastic cement.

❏ Plywood is cut out 1½ in. to 2 in. for ridge vents as specified.

❏ Ridge vents are installed according to plans and specs.

❏ Ridge vents have end caps installed.

❏ Ridge cap shingles are properly installed.

❏ Fireplace chimneys have chimney crickets on the back side where required.

❏ Fireplace chimneys have step flashing and counter flashing installed around the chimney opening according to proper construction procedures.

❏ All scrap shingles are properly disposed of and excess shingles are stacked for return to the supplier.

Signature: _____

The measurements given represent standards used by one construction company; they may not be suited to all construction companies in all regions. Consult your local building codes and individual company standards before adapting and using this checklist.

Figure 3.9 Drywall Quality Checklist

Job number: _____   Date: _____

❏ Attic access installed properly.

❏ Factory edge on drywall at attic access opening returns.

❏ All appropriate drywall installed.

❏ Check walls for smooth finish everywhere.

❏ *All* holes and cracks are filled so as not to show when painted.

❏ Check corners for smooth finish everywhere.

❏ Check for loose nails or pops.

❏ Exterior walls are screwed in place.

❏ Interior walls are glued and screwed properly.

❏ Nails are used only to tack drywall in place.

❏ Check around windows for proper fit and finish.

❏ Windows and doors are caulked.

❏ Check around outlets boxes for good fit.

❏ Walls and ceilings are textured as required. Texture is uniform in appearance.

❏ Drywall is installed vertically at slit-level openings.

❏ Fire walls are properly sealed and fire-taped as required by local and CABO code.

❏ Surfaces are sanded as needed.

❏ Surfaces are clean.

❏ Excess drywall was returned for credit.

❏ Scrap material placed in the scrap pile.

❏ Floors were scraped and house swept and left broom-clean by the drywaller.

❏ No electrical outlet boxes or wires are concealed.

Signature: _____

The measurements given represent standards used by one construction company; they may not be suited to all construction companies in all regions. Consult your local building codes and individual company standards before adapting and using this checklist.

Figure 3.10 Pre Walk-Through Quality Checklist

Job number: _____   Date: _____

Exterior

❑ Check to make sure all stoop and garage forms are removed.

❑ Grade away from house 6 in. in 10 ft.

❑ Final grade smooth and back fill settled properly.

❑ Loose concrete cleaned up and hauled off.

❑ Hose bibs work.

❑ No broken windows.

❑ Brick cleaned.

❑ Check gas meter and electrical meter for proper connection and seal.

❑ Make sure downspout color and placement are per contract and print.

❑ Check for valley guards.

❑ Gutters and downspouts properly installed.

❑ All exterior trim installed properly.

❑ Shutters installed securely.

❑ Caulk family room/utility room windows at brick.

❑ Walk roof.

❑ Shingles installed correctly, none blown off.

❑ Roof jacks (roof vent collars) caulked or sealed with plastic cement.

❑ Windows installed securely, operate correctly, and caulked including top.

❑ Screens installed.

❑ Siding nailed properly (loosely nailed); examine for bulges.

❑ Check drip cap over gable windows and garage doors.

❑ Trim nailed and caulked properly.

❑ Deck installed and nailed properly.

❑ Steps and railings secured.

❑ Exterior locks working.

❑ Exterior doors properly hung.

❑ Weather stripping and threshold installed and adjusted so no air passes.

❑ Garage doors properly installed and operating.

❑ Site is clean.

Interior

❑ Check subfloor for squeaks.

❑ All doors installed properly, are plumb, open freely, and don't close by themselves.

❑ All bypass and bifold doors are plumb and operate properly in their track.

❑ All doors clear the carpet.

❑ Door bumpers installed.

❑ Base joints fit tightly.

❑ All shelving installed properly.

❑ Shelf rods installed.

❑ Drywall in garage is hung and taped (if required).

❑ Check chips or scratches in wall. Repair if necessary.

❑ Check countertops for chips and scratches.

❑ Adequate insulation properly installed in attic.

❑ Attic access installed and insulated properly.

❑ Outlets and switches installed—no holes in sheetrock.

❑ Check lights and outlets for operation.

❑ Test all fans to make sure they work.

❑ Test garbage disposal, if applicable.

❑ Test dishwasher for function.

❑ Test oven and stove make sure they operate properly.

❑ All light fixtures must have bulbs in them and work.

❑ All electrical trim in place.

❑ All smoke alarms function.

❑ All heat registers in place or available for installation.

❑ Clean filter in furnace.

❑ Furnace turned on in the winter.

❑ A/C on in the summer.

(continued)

Figure 3.10 Pre Walk-Through Quality Checklist (continued)

- ❏ Thermostat set at 70°F.
- ❏ Tubs installed properly and caulked.
- ❏ Test whirlpools.
- ❏ Plumbing fixtures installed properly.
- ❏ Turn on water in all sinks to assure function.
- ❏ Turn on hot water at all sinks to assure hot water reaches all fixtures.
- ❏ Check for leaks.
- ❏ Flush toilets.
- ❏ Floor drains have water in traps.
- ❏ Plumbing access panels installed where required.
- ❏ Bath hardware securely installed.
- ❏ Mirrors securely installed.
- ❏ Shower doors installed and caulked (where applicable).
- ❏ Appliances installed and working properly.
- ❏ Check cabinets and tops to color chart.
- ❏ Check backsplash type, full or 4 in.
- ❏ Cabinets properly installed. Cabinet doors are plumb.
- ❏ Cabinet doors and drawers operate properly. Open all cabinets and eliminate squeaks.
- ❏ Cabinet trim properly installed.
- ❏ Countertops installed and properly caulked.
- ❏ Check soffit reveal.
- ❏ Check linen closet shelving for proper installation.
- ❏ Check all floor coverings (where applicable) for proper installation and any damage.
- ❏ Rails and balusters securely fastened.
- ❏ Try all the windows to make sure they open without binding.
- ❏ Caulk around basement windows.

- ❏ Garage and basement floor free from taping mud on floor.
- ❏ Interior generally clean.
- ❏ Floors swept clean.
- ❏ Handrails and/or guardrails are installed and properly secured on basement stairs.
- ❏ Bridging is properly installed and repaired as needed.
- ❏ Check for missing insulation in basement and floor joists, especially in cantilevers.
- ❏ Check basement walls for damage.
- ❏ Sump drainage line is sealed with mortar inside and out.
- ❏ Clean out sump and secure the lid.
- ❏ Check all sump, water, and drain lines that go through the foundation to make sure they are sealed.
- ❏ Basement cleaned up, floor swept clean or washed if needed.
- ❏ All parts of the house must appear clean and free from construction debris.
- ❏ All excess material neatly stacked in the garage or returned for credit.
- ❏ Basement windows caulked.
- ❏ Review the contracts and check all change orders to make sure they are completed.
- ❏ Manuals for appliances and systems together for owner.

Signature: _____

The measurements given represent standards used by one construction company; they may not be suited to all construction companies in all regions. Consult your local building codes and individual company standards before adapting and using this checklist.

Chapter 4

Budget Control

Introduction

Building a project within the established budget is a primary goal of every superintendent. Therefore, every project should have an established budget before a single nail is hammered—or even ordered. This budget is normally derived directly from the detailed estimate of the house. Production builders may determine budgets from accounting records for the same model (when the same type of house will be built). The budget can be broken into two parts:

- summary of all of the major costs involved in the building the home
- detailed account of all items (both the quantity and the itemized cost) which are required to build the house

A detailed estimate of all of the costs associated with building the house is needed so that you can keep track of the costs as they occur and take corrective action whenever budgeted and actual values differ.

Corrective action may be in the form of some procedural or personnel change, or simply a recognition that the budget is in error and needs to be adjusted on future jobs.

Establishing the Budget

The way the budget will be subdivided will depend in part on the sophistication of the company and on the kinds of homes being built. For example, different work areas may be grouped as follows:

- job overhead
- sitework
- foundations
- masonry

- wood framing
- roofing and flashing
- exterior siding and brick
- heating and air conditioning
- plumbing
- electrical
- insulation
- drywall
- interior wood trim
- painting
- cabinets
- floor covering
- appliances
- landscaping, walks, and driveways

All builders should develop a detailed chart of accounts, taking into account the company's needs and type of construction. The chart of accounts should be consistent from one job to the next and flexible enough to handle the different types of work the company performs, from new construction to remodeling projects. A chart of accounts can be derived directly from the detailed estimate of the house, including construction materials, subcontracts, direct labor, maintenance and repair expense, and field overhead/office expenses. Using the estimates for each category of work, set up budget line items in the same sequence as the steps of construction. Budget categories should match the cost of sales accounts in your chart of accounts. An excellent sample chart of accounts for builders and remodelers was originally proposed by Lee Evans in the 1960s. Over the years it has been modified and updated several times by the business management committee of NAHB. The complete NAHB Chart of Accounts is found in NAHB's *Accounting and Financial Management for Builders and Remodelers*. All residential builders and remodelers should take advantage of this excellent source of information. It was developed by builders for builders and provides an excellent format for establishing a chart of accounts.

In deciding how to subdivide the work areas, keep in mind that expenditures for each work item must be easily measurable. Another good rule is to lump together similar items that occur within the same time frame. For example, it would be unwise to group rough grading and finish grading or framing lumber and trim material, even though these materials may come from the same vendor. Comparisons against the budget need to be made as quickly as possible after each delivery of step in the work to see if the job is still within the targeted budget. Timely checking of expenditures against the budget will often allow you to take corrective steps before it's too late.

You will want to ensure that the numbers used in estimating, accounting, and budgeting procedures are as accurate as possible. Most building companies should employ an integrated numbering system for accounting, estimating, purchasing, and other functions. If you have in-house employees who perform direct labor (carpenters, masons, and so forth), maintaining accurate time sheets relative to each work category and keeping up with materials moved from one job to another are essential to determining whether or not a job is profitable.

Material Control

In order to control the budget, you must take pains to control the materials used in the construction of homes. Proper utilization of materials is crucial to any construction company's cost-effective operation and is therefore an important superintendent responsibility. Material control is a function of seven basic building activities:

- value engineering and planning
- completing specifications
- ensuring accurate contracts
- purchasing
- scheduling deliveries
- providing proper storage and care of materials
- avoiding material waste and misuse

Introduction to Value Engineering

In the home building industry, value engineering is an effort to get the most for consumers' dollars without sacrificing quality or the function for which the building is intended. The basis for value engineering in the industry centers on optimum value engineering (OVE) systems, such as the system developed in conjunction with the U.S. Department of Housing and Urban Development and the NAHB Research Center.

OVE systems offer many useful and money-saving guidelines for the utilization and conservation of materials. In addition, when OVE principles are applied systematically and appropriately, they produce a better and more economical product—one that serves its function better in many cases than a house built in a more traditional manner. For example, studies have shown that placing studs and floor joists 24 inches on center and aligning them with the roof trusses (which are normally 24 inches on center), not only conserves materials, but also increases the structural stability of the building (see Figure 4.1).

As mentioned earlier, OVE is a group of closely related cost-saving methods. It begins during the planning process, takes into account alternative construction techniques, and is carefully integrated with the construction process so that all phases of construction effectively complement each other. While OVE techniques do not require detailed engineering analysis, professional engineering advice may sometimes prove helpful in making the most of OVE concepts. Having an engineer design or evaluate each house, however, is unnecessary; concepts that prove valid in one instance can be applied in similar situations on other jobs.

Value Engineering: Three Steps

Value engineering is based upon the following three simple steps:

- gathering information
- identifying, analyzing, and evaluating alternatives
- selecting and implementing the best alternatives

Figure 4.1 Comparison of 16-inch and 24-inch On-Center Framing

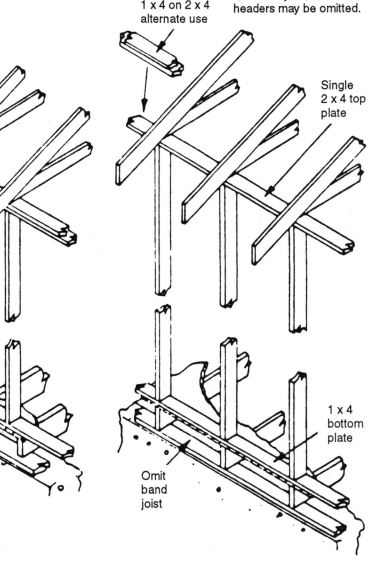

**Standard framing
16 inches on center**
Truss, stud, and joist may
or may not be in line.

**OVE framing
24 inches on center**
Truss, stud, and joist are
directly in line. Load is
supplied more efficiently.
In addition to savings on
top and bottom plates
and band joist, structural
headers may be omitted.

Double
2 x 4 top
plate

1 x 4 on 2 x 4
alternate use

Single
2 x 4 top
plate

Band
joist

2 x 4
bottom
plate

1 x 4
bottom
plate

Omit
band
joist

Gathering Information. First, determine the worth of an item used in construction in dollar amounts. In some cases, an item may have aesthetic value but little or no structural value. The value must then be determined by the individual purchasing the product. For example, a home buyer may wish to have a certain type of window placed in his or her home out of personal preference, perhaps because the window is particularly attractive. This type of consideration is entirely different from purchasing windows to achieve energy efficiency.

Identifying, Analyzing, and Evaluating Alternatives. Identifying cost-saving techniques involves generating new, cost-saving ideas to serve necessary functions within the house being built. For example, many of the newest, most innovative approaches focus on efficient floor plans and products that make the most of fewer square feet while producing a home that meets the needs of potential buyers. Analysis of new approaches should be both systematic and objective. In order to determine the advantages and disadvantages of an alternative approach, each must be evaluated and tested to ensure feasibility. Keep in mind that customer acceptance must be a key factor in determining feasibility. It does no good to develop a newer, cheaper, better way of doing something if the consumer doesn't want it or won't buy it. Estimate an alternative's value by asking: What does it cost overall, and what are the potential savings? Other factors you should consider when evaluating alternatives include aesthetics, durability, marketability, and lifetime cost with maintenance (as distinct from unit-in-place cost).

Selecting and Implementing Alternatives. Once the alternatives have been evaluated, some ideas will fail to meet a home's functional requirements and will be rejected outright. Other alternatives may appear to have great potential but require additional information before you can reach a final decision. Such alternatives should be reserved for further research. Select those ideas that offer the greatest savings while still maintaining the functional qualities required. Once a final decision has been reached, all costs should be recorded and monitored, including installation, maintenance, and use of the product or technique, to ensure that the anticipated savings are realized.

Completing Specifications

Specifications can be quite a challenge for a superintendent, but at some point you have to decide what materials and how much of each item you are going to need to build the home. You may be provided with only a foundation plan, floor plan, and elevation and asked to construct a house from this sketchy information. You might as well establish specifications up front and set the expectation level of your customer before you start construction.

Proper use of adequate plans and specifications can eliminate most problems before they begin. By clarifying the homeowner's desires (in the case of custom work) and completing the specifications, builders and superintendents can improve efficiency on the jobsite and make intelligent, accurate decisions when submitting bids for custom work. Therefore, regardless of who furnishes the plans and specifications, make certain that every item is specified or that at least an allowance is agreed upon. When setting these allowances, it may be tempting to recommend low values in order to make the overall price more attractive. However, setting realistic initial allowances helps keep the home buyer happy by minimizing the possibility of later surprises and their accompanying higher costs. This professional approach will help to keep your company's good reputation intact.

Ensuring Accurate Contracts

Legally, anything that is not part of the contract is not required of the builder. In an effort to maintain good working relationships with their customers, many builders will give in to the wishes of a buyer rather than face an argument. However, you should keep in mind that if a buyer has contracted to buy a "Chevrolet" house, you should not be forced to deliver a "Cadillac" house at the same price. Only by specifying what is wanted up front and in writing can home buyers and builders reach agreement.

The same holds true for your subcontractors. You should obtain a written subcontract agreement for each subcontractor. These don't need to be complex legal documents drawn up by a lawyer. They can be simple agreements written in your own words. Each agreement should outline what you expect and what you are willing to accept from your subcontractors. It should include such details as how and when you expect to make payment, cleanup procedures, OSHA compliance, and so forth. NAHB has materials that can help you develop subcontract agreements.

Purchasing

Purchasing is one of the most overlooked management tools available to small-volume builders. Building houses without purchase orders is like framing houses without power nailing guns. It can be done, but it's really hard to make money. An effective purchasing system can save you a lot of money and reduces the time your workers and subs spend running around town picking up materials that either were not ordered or have not yet been delivered to the site.

Studies show that by implementing a good purchasing system, including the use of formal purchase orders for all material and subcontracts, you can raise your profit margin by several percentage points. One particularly well-managed company implemented a purchase order system and increased its bottom-line profit margin from 9 percent to over 16 percent in one year. That's a 78 percent increase in profits in one year!

Because superintendents and the crews directly under them actually use the construction materials, they can monitor day-to-day material needs, including what specific materials are needed and where they should be placed on the jobsite. Therefore, while office staff can initiate purchase orders and send them to suppliers to authorize purchases, you as the superintendent should place the final will-call order and request delivery.

The first step in implementing a purchase order system is to complete or refer to the detailed estimate created for the home. The estimate must contain absolutely everything required to build the home. From a completed estimate, purchase orders can be generated for everything from the excavator to the floor coverings. In most cases, generating purchase orders is automatic. If you have a computerized estimating system integrated with a purchasing system, then your computer can generate and print purchase orders for you.

The next step is to review all of the purchase orders. Because the superintendent is responsible for building the job and coordinating the subcontractors, you need to review the estimate to make sure that the purchase orders contain everything and that the proper subcontractors have been assigned to the job.

The approved purchase orders are then mailed to all subcontractors before construction begins (Figure 4.2 shows the paper flow of a purchase order system). One medium-sized builder who works on scattered sites throughout the state includes the necessary copies of the plans for each sub and a map to each job. Sending out purchase orders in advance leads to many good things:

- Once accepted, the purchase order becomes a legal contract which obligates the vendor to supply the material or labor specified at the price indicated.
- The vendor is notified that you need the material specified and will generally reserve materials in short supply for your particular job.
- Prices are pretty well fixed. Even when there are price increases during construction, most suppliers and subcontractors will hold the prices specified in the purchase order. Because the purchase order is a contract, the vendor will adhere to the price more readily than if you only requested an estimate. In essence, you have already agreed to purchase the material. You simply are delaying delivery until the proper time.
- Your subcontractors all know what you are going to build far in advance and they can begin to plan schedules and teams accordingly.
- The purchase of materials and supplies is limited to only those who are authorized by the original estimate.

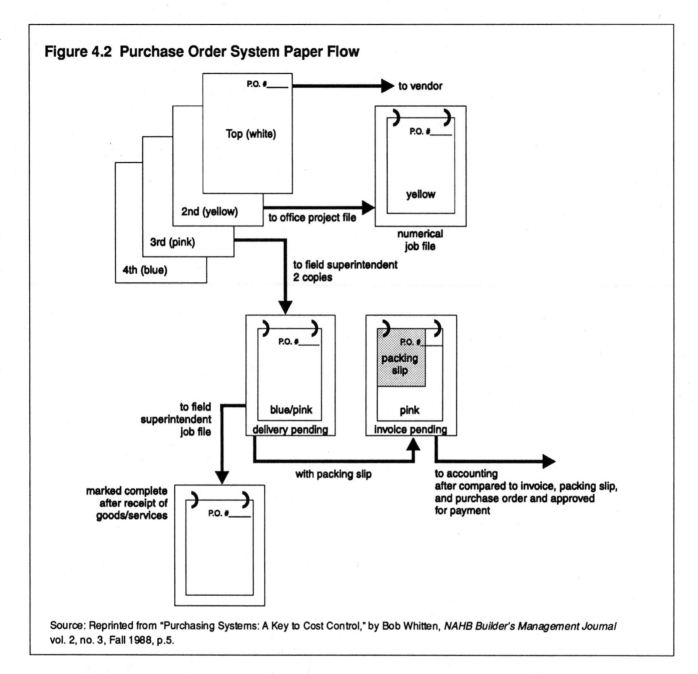

Figure 4.2 Purchase Order System Paper Flow

Source: Reprinted from "Purchasing Systems: A Key to Cost Control," by Bob Whitten, *NAHB Builder's Management Journal* vol. 2, no. 3, Fall 1988, p.5.

- Items not included in the original budget can be easily tracked (see Handling Budget Variances).
- Ordering and delivery of materials are much simpler. You just request delivery of a particular purchase order.

When the material is delivered, the superintendent or subcontractor checks the delivery to make sure it is complete and is of the appropriate quality. When the subcontractor completes the work, it is approved for payment. In many cases, it is not even necessary to have the subcontractor or supplier issue an invoice or statement. The superintendent approves the material or subcontract work for payment directly. The accounting department makes payment directly from the purchase order. This eliminates a lot of paperwork, and the subcontractor or supplier is paid more quickly.

Handling Budget Variances

A variance is any cost that was not included in the original estimate or budget. Obviously, variances should be avoided. You can reduce budget variances if you:

- build well-designed homes with complete plans and specifications
- obtain accurate estimates of material and labor
- maintain a good purchase order system
- schedule just-in-time material deliveries
- count and inspect materials for quality and correct quantity
- train subcontractors to use materials properly
- use cut sheets to show subs how you propose to use materials
- negotiate long-term pricing for materials and labor
- maintain proper security on the job to avoid theft and vandalism
- take precautions to protect materials from weather
- reduce or eliminate change orders
- closely supervise quality on the job
- protect previously completed work

We all know that it is almost impossible to build a house without any variances. When a variance does occur, it is important to identify the cause and keep track of it in order to reduce variances in the future. This is done through the use of a variance purchase order (VPO). Just as a purchase order authorizes the purchase of materials and subcontracted work that were included in the original estimate, a VPO authorizes purchase of materials or subcontracted work that was not included in the original estimate. The concept of the variance purchase order system has been promoted for many years by Lee Evans. While it requires a fair amount of discipline, using a variance purchase order system results in savings on the purchase of unwarranted items or subcontracted work.

Essentially a VPO must be filled out for anything which was not included in the original estimate. In most cases, the VPO is filled out by the superintendent in the field and authorizes delivery of materials or performance of work. A VPO contains four sections:

- identification of pertinent job information
- listing of the materials or work to be performed

- explanation of the cause of the variance
- identification of the action needed to avoid the variance in the future

The completed VPO is then approved for payment by the superintendent's supervisor. A VPO allows you to keep track of the cause and amount of variances on each job and to compare them from one job to another, from one subcontractor to another, and even from one company to another. If you can identify the common causes of variances, you can take the necessary steps to avoid them or at least reduce their number and dollar amount.

Scheduling Deliveries

Most of what you need to know about scheduling deliveries is basic common sense: Materials should be delivered when they are needed and stored close to where they will be used. Proper scheduling of material deliveries cuts down on both wasted time and wasted materials. Avoid scheduling material deliveries just prior to weekends, since most jobsite theft occurs on weekends and holidays.

Have a Specified Delivery Site. Identify each jobsite with a conspicuous job number. Putting that same job number on all delivery tickets helps to ensure that materials arrive at the correct location. You should make certain that delivered materials are stacked with the materials to be used first on top of the pile. One way to accomplish this arrangement is to list those items required on top of the pile at the *bottom* of the purchase order. These materials will likely be loaded onto the truck last and therefore end up on the top of the pile. With each purchase order, you may want to include a simple plot plan showing the exact location on the lot where the materials should be placed. Then identify the location on the site with a small sign that simply says "**Lumber Drop Here**," for example. Most drivers will deliver the materials to the location indicated, and workers will not waste time trying to find what they need.

Conducting Delivery Inspections. Materials should always be inspected on the jobsite upon delivery. Problems often occur when deliveries are made to a jobsite where no one is present to direct the driver and immediately inspect the materials. Therefore, if possible, the superintendent or another responsible worker should be available at the site when a delivery is due. If that is not possible, you or the subcontractor who will use the material should check each load of material as soon as possible before it is disturbed to make sure it is complete and in good condition.

While many materials such as lumber have been inspected by the manufacturer before shipment, many latent defects can occur by the time materials reach the jobsite. For example, lumber can warp, crack, and split, making it difficult or impossible to use in many cases. In keeping with lumber grading rules common in the industry, as much as 5 percent of lumber in a delivery may be out of specification. While some of this lumber might be used as blocking, much of it cannot be used and should be returned. Your thorough inspection can prevent the use and subsequent rejection of defective materials after installation or at inspection time. In addition, rejecting an unacceptable floor joist before installation is much easier and less expensive than having to replace it after installation. Rejected materials should therefore be located, clearly marked in such a way that they cannot be used, and placed away from other materials to prevent confusion between acceptable and unacceptable materials.

Inspection of materials at the jobsite will also detect any defects resulting from storage, transportation, or unloading. Proper inspection now will alleviate the problem of arguing with suppliers later over any damage. Keep in mind that suppliers are often the victims of unjust claims for defective materials when, in fact, the problem occurred as a result of product misuse or abuse on the part of the subcontractor or workers during construction. Suppliers have consequently become more sensitive about complaints from superintendents concerning damaged materials. Early inspection upon delivery should limit the room for argument on both sides.

Most suppliers are honest and will not intentionally short a builder. However, employees are human and often forget a particular item or leave materials back at the warehouse instead of delivering them to the jobsite. This problem is common for small items such as nails, bolts, and adhesive, particularly in large orders where items are easily overlooked. Therefore, inspect carefully to ensure that all materials have been delivered as ordered.

Finally, you should always be conscious of your right and your obligation to reject faulty materials. Most material suppliers will stand behind their products and substitute good materials for inferior ones, usually at no cost to you.

Providing Proper Storage and Care

Materials on the jobsite are often wasted because of improper storage and care. For example, materials can be ruined by mud or snow during extreme weather conditions. In the hot weather common in many parts of the country, exposed lumber can dry out and warp; when shipped to hot, dry climates, even kiln-dried lumber can be ruined through careless storage—or lack of storage. Materials subject to deterioration should therefore be covered at all times. In addition, a bundle of lumber should be used as soon as possible after it is opened to prevent warping and twisting. Twenty guidelines for the conservation and care of building materials, prepared by Lee Evans in his *Quality in Construction*, are offered in Figure 4.3.

Avoiding Material Waste and Misuse

The large scrap piles found on most construction sites are the most obvious symptom of the growing problem of material waste in the construction industry. Taking the time to preplan your use of materials can eliminate a substantial amount of this waste. Spend a little extra time at the drafting table and graphically depict how materials are to be installed. The resulting drawings can communicate to your workers and subs the exact manner in which materials are to be used—eliminating waste and saving money. Many builders also distribute copies of approved construction methods and procedures, further stipulating the efficient use of materials. In addition, giving your framing subcontractor's crew a copy of the estimate without prices is a good practice. The estimate normally indicates the type of material to be used and its intended

Figure 4.3 Guidelines for Conservation and Care of Building Materials*

1. Can materials be ordered in smaller quantities to reduce exposure time?
2. Can the supplier load them so that materials used first are on the top instead of the bottom of the load? (Because of the time saved, builders may be able to afford to pay something extra for this service, especially if they use their own crews or can negotiate with subcontractors to recover some of the time savings.)
3. Can the superintendent do anything else to improve planning load composition, size, or delivery spotting to avoid extra handling?
4. Can any kind of temporary cover such as plastic be used? (Provide shelter but do not make a sweat box by covering materials too tightly.)
5. Can the load be banded in several batches rather than in one big load?
6. Is a spot by the foundation prepared for the load? Does it provide drainage? Are skids provided to keep the load off the ground? (Ideally it should be up 6 inches, and in bad weather, polyethylene laid below the load to prevent moisture rise.)
7. Are asphalt roofing materials stored flat? (Curved and buckled shingles create an unsightly roof.)
8. Can any of the load delivery spots be covered with stone or paved? (In multifamily projects, paving or stone is desirable because subsequent handling can be done with lift trucks, but doing that requires much planning and scheduling.)
9. Are siding materials stored so that they will not be scratched or damaged?
10. Can scheduling be changed to prevent deliveries from being exposed to weather for more than a day or two?
11. Can theft of site materials be reduced? Can materials be nailed down or locked up before dark? Will reducing deliveries to one-day requirements help? Can materials be banded, wired, or nailed together or marked to help recover or identify them for prosecution? Can superintendents and builders cooperate to do anything in the way of rewards for information?
12. What can be done to prevent vandalism?
13. Can superintendents train in-house labor and subcontractor workers to take better care of materials? (Stacks that are torn into and scattered deteriorate rapidly.)
14. Is too much material ordered for a particular unit or building resulting in waste, downgrading, or rehandling?
15. Is a place prepared for temporary storage of trim and similar materials so that they are dry, straight, and not disturbed?
16. Is each unit dried-in quickly enough? Is siding applied soon enough to prevent water drainage in the house?
17. Is temporary drainage provided and directed away from the house?
18. Can some deliveries and phases of construction be rescheduled so that materials are not damaged by workers? (For example, lay flooring materials late in the process. Don't deliver doors, door frames, and windows until the unit is ready for installation. These items, as well as finishes, are damaged when workers move them.)
19. Can protective coverings be provided for such items as bath tubs, flooring materials, plastic laminate tops, and appliances?
20. Can temporary furnace heat be provided to help dry out the house and to prevent moisture buildup in flooring materials, trim, and paneling?

* Adapted from Lee S. Evans, *Quality in Construction* (Washington, DC: National Association of Home Builders, 1974) p. 51.

use. For example, a 2x4x14 could be used for a myriad of things from wall plates to rafter tails. How is a subcontractor or framer supposed to know what all of the material in a pile of lumber is designated for without a copy of the estimate? By referring to the estimate, the carpenter will know that that 2x4x14 is to be used as a fly rafter.

Labor Control

Many builders feel they can do little to control the cost of materials, so instead they focus on labor costs as the primary avenue for potential savings. This greater direct control of labor may have been possible in the past, when builders employed crews for large portion of the work. However, with the trend toward the increased use of subcontractors, labor efficiency is now under the direct control of the subcontractor. Of course, the superintendent who discovers ways for a subcontractor to increase productivity may lower costs for future jobs. In addition, you can help to keep costs down by watching carefully for subcontractor errors that may be properly backcharged to the responsible sub. Backcharging a sub can be a tricky process. As often as not, a backcharge on one job becomes a price increase in the next job. It has been the experience of many builders that backcharges simply don't work very well. It is a lot better to educate subs and cooperate with them than to blame and alienate them.

Chapter 5

Schedule Control

Introduction

Completing a job on schedule is another primary goal of the superintendent. With all the interrelated functions that must be accomplished in proper sequence, construction must progress in the most efficient and economical manner possible. Effective scheduling is the key to this efficiency and contributes directly to the success of many builders in today's competitive marketplace. Many contracts are awarded as much on the basis of ability of the builder to complete the project in a timely manner as on overall price.

Any builder will tell you it is easier to build a house with a good written schedule than it is without one. A formal, written schedule allows you to build a house with less effort because it organizes the work sequence in much the same way a good set of plans and specifications organizes what is to be built. Because a formal schedule makes the work easier, you can build more houses with less effort than was possible using informal scheduling or no scheduling at all.

Why Schedule?

Many builders and superintendents who currently "fly by the seat of their pants" may wonder why they need to adopt a more formal scheduling approach. The reasons are many:

- Scheduling a project is one of the two most important things you need to do before you start a project. Most successful builders wouldn't start a project without a detailed estimate of all of the things that contribute to the cost of a project. By the same token, it is essential to plan out the sequence and interaction of all of the activities that must be performed to com-

plete the home. Scheduling allows you to build the project in your head and solve most of the problems with building a home before they occur.

- Scheduling allows you to give adequate notice to each subcontractor well in advance of when they are needed so they can plan their schedules. If subcontractors know you need them well in advance, your chances of having them on the job and completing the project on time increase substantially. Good communication is the key to better subcontractor management. A good schedule can be the tool you need to communicate effectively with subcontractors.
- Scheduling can help to level out the up-and-down cycles typical in the construction industry by reducing slack time and increasing overall productivity.
- A good schedule will point out bottlenecks where labor, equipment, and materials are too tightly scheduled and also occasions where resources are spread too thin.
- Scheduling provides options when unexpected delays occur due to equipment breakdowns, subcontractors failing to show up, or bad weather. Flexibility in work assignments is also improved.
- The biggest reason to use formalized scheduling systems is because they work! Formalized scheduling gives you a powerful tool that allows you to manage the project more effectively.

Getting Started

It is possible for a superintendent to use a schedule effectively without being able to create or draw one. However, knowing how to create a formal schedule on paper should help you to use and understand the schedule even better. Since the intent of this chapter is to provide an overview of basic scheduling methods and their benefits, many of the steps necessary to creating a schedule are provided. Superintendents and builders interested in learning more about formal scheduling procedures should see *Scheduling Residential Construction for Builders and Remodelers* from the National Association of Home Builders.

Scheduling Methods

The type of scheduling system a building company uses depends on several interrelated factors:

- size of building company
- volume of work accomplished
- type of construction
- owner's or architect's requirements (in custom work)
- project location
- competition
- project size
- project complexity
- extent of subcontracted work
- capacity of the superintendent
- work load (current and anticipated)
- past experience with schedules
- contract provisions
- computer capability

While many scheduling methods are in use in the construction industry today, including many computer applications, this discussion will concentrate on two of the most practical for either manual or computer use: the bar chart and the Critical Path Method (CPM) or logic diagram.

Scheduling Phases

There are six steps to formal scheduling for both the bar chart and CPM methods:

- Planning: The project is broken down into different activities.
- Scheduling: The duration of each individual activity is established.
- Sequencing: The interrelationship and sequence of the activities are determined.

- Communicating: The overall schedule is depicted and communicated to the various participants.
- Monitoring: The superintendent uses the written schedule to manage the project.
- Updating: The schedule is updated as the project progresses.

Sequencing Activities

Work should flow without interruption. To achieve this flow, activities must be properly sequenced from the start. You should keep in mind that two or more distinct parts of a particular task occurring at different times in the job need to be scheduled as separate activities. For example, the electrical work should be divided into electrical rough-in and electrical trim-out.

An activity is a single work step that has a recognizable beginning and end and requires time for its accomplishment. As you consider the various construction activities, you may want to organize them according to the following categories:

- Area of responsibility or craft: Activities can be organized according to the subcontractors who will perform them. Subs may appear more then once if they are performing more than one activity, or if they are performing work at different stages.
- Structural elements: Activities using the same subcontractor, such as footings and concrete flatwork, may be further separated when they represent different structural elements completed at different times.
- Location on project: Similar activities, such as interior concrete, floors, and exterior flatwork may be considered separate activities because they are performed in different locations, usually at different times.
- Material vendor: Materials supplied by different vendors, such as garage doors and interior doors, or trusses and other framing lumber, should usually be considered separate activities.

Your final activities list should be arranged in approximate sequential order. Three crucial questions should be answered in order to develop an accurate sequence:

- Which, if any, activities must precede this activity?
- Which, if any, activities must follow this activity?
- Which activities can be conducted simultaneously?

Several constraints can also affect sequence, including the following:

- Physical (or logical) constraints: Practical constraints involve such factors as labor or equipment availability, construction methods, and safety constraints.
- Practical constraints: Practical constraints are either an economic or safety consideration. What is the safest, most economical way to accomplish a task? Failure to consider such constraints can be disastrous to an otherwise adequate job schedule.
- Managerial constraints: Management may require that a project be constructed in a specific way. Such constraints may be a direct result of the home buyer's desires, the company's financial requirements, computer or accounting constraints, the availability of competent managerial control, or simply managerial preference. These constraints are real, and you should be prepared to work within the guidelines established.

Determining Activity Duration

Assigning the time required for construction activities is usually based on the superintendent's experience and knowledge of local conditions. You should begin by obtaining a time estimate from each subcontractor. Sometimes, busy subs may put a small token work force to "stake a claim" on your jobsite while finishing up work for another builder. A good estimate of time requirements up front should help to curtail this behavior.

Several rules will help you in estimating activity durations:

- Evaluate each activity independent of all others.
- Obtain information from subcontractors on time durations.
- Assume a normal work force for your crew and for subcontractors. Avoid overloading

your work force to make the activity duration match the overall time allotted.
- Assume normal production rates for the time of year in which the work will be performed.
- Assume a normal work day. Overtime or multiple-shift work can be entered into the process later if needed. While a certain portion of the work may be accelerated for a limited time to meet a crisis or solve a particular problem, this solution should be the exception rather than the rule.
- Use consistent time units of working days and half days.
- Be as accurate as is practicable. Do not overestimate time durations in an attempt to make the schedule more manageable, or underestimate in order to keep it tight. Work tends to take as much time as you allow, so avoid putting too much padding into a schedule.

No activity should be scheduled for less than half a day. Any task taking less time should be rounded up to a half day. For example, to get to a job and set the grade stakes may take only an hour, but a half day should be scheduled. Likewise, any activity that is expected to take five or six hours, such as grading the lot, should be scheduled as a whole day.

The Bar Chart

Scheduling with a bar chart allows all those involved in the construction process to see easily where their task falls on the construction time line.

Planning the Bar Chart

The bar chart is the more basic of the two scheduling methods offered here, requiring only that all construction activities be sequenced, and that a time duration be estimated for each.

Scheduling with the Bar Chart

A bar chart puts construction activities in a calendar format. Figure 5.1 shows a complete list of activities with projected time slots. The bars on the calendar portion of the chart indicate when the activities are to occur. According to this sample chart, this simple house should be completed in 72 days.

Figure 5.1 The Bar Chart

One of the biggest advantages to a bar chart is its simple visual clarity. When an activity will begin and end is easily seen and understood. You and your workers and subs can see at a glance how the work will progress.

Monitoring the Bar Chart

Unfortunately, the strengths of the bar chart method can also become weaknesses when monitoring activities. A bar chart cannot show the complex interdependence between various activities. For example, landscaping could be completed as early as the brick or siding and exterior concrete are complete or wait until just before you complete the house. However, some activities are critical to timely completion of the project; that is, they absolutely must happen at a particular time or the project will be delayed. Framing, for example, is almost always a critical activity. Pouring the basement floor, on the other hand, can be done as soon as the foundation is complete and the underground plumbing is installed. Or it could wait until the house is framed and dried in.

A bar chart will not normally show the float, or slack time, in noncritical activities. By the same token, a bar chart does not show what happens when a particular activity is delayed. Suppose, for example, that the burgundy tub you ordered for a custom home is delayed. What other activities are affected? Will insulation or drywall be delayed? You really can't tell what impact a delay will have on other activities on a bar chart. Therefore, you may wish to reserve the bar chart method for use as a general planning tool when a graphic display of the interrelationships is unnecessary.

The Critical Path Method

Unlike the bar chart method, the Critical Path Method of scheduling identifies those activities that *must* be completed on schedule in order for the job to finish on time and graphically shows the interaction between different activities.

Planning the CPM Diagram

When planning a CPM diagram, the sequencing and duration activities are much the same as those for a bar chart. The difference is in how the CPM diagram relates activities' sequence and duration to each other. In a CPM diagram, a circle (or node) represents work to be performed, and the relationships between activities are depicted by an arrow (see Figure 5.2). Each circle contains a number identifying each activity. For example, activity 39 represents "cabinet installation."

Scheduling with a CPM Diagram

Following a CPM diagram is relatively simple. A basic rule states that *all* activities coming into a particular activity must be completed before that activity can begin. For example, on our sample house shown in Figure 5.2, it was determined that wood trim would be installed after the interior painting was complete.

You can easily follow the superintendent's scheduling approach by viewing the schedule network. First, the scheduler determines and plans the first job: Laying out the home is the first activity. With the lot laid out, you can begin to excavate. After the excavation is complete, footing continues, and so on. After dampproofing is complete, three tasks can begin:

- brace foundation
- foundation inspection
- cure foundation

Notice that, after the framing is completed, there is a construction manager inspection, then the roofing, HVAC rough-in, rough plumbing, and electrical rough-in may be done. Also notice that, as these three jobs are completed, the inspections immediately follow.

Monitoring the CPM Diagram

During the monitoring phase, the superintendent can use the CPM diagram to the greatest advantage. One of the most effective monitoring techniques involves highlighting activities or parts of activities with a colored pen or highlighting marker. By doing so, you will be able to tell at a glance which activities are underway—and what is coming up next. If you are using one of the many computer programs available to do your scheduling, updating the schedule may be as simple as indicating on the schedule that the activity is complete, or 40 percent complete,

Figure 5.2 The CPM Diagram

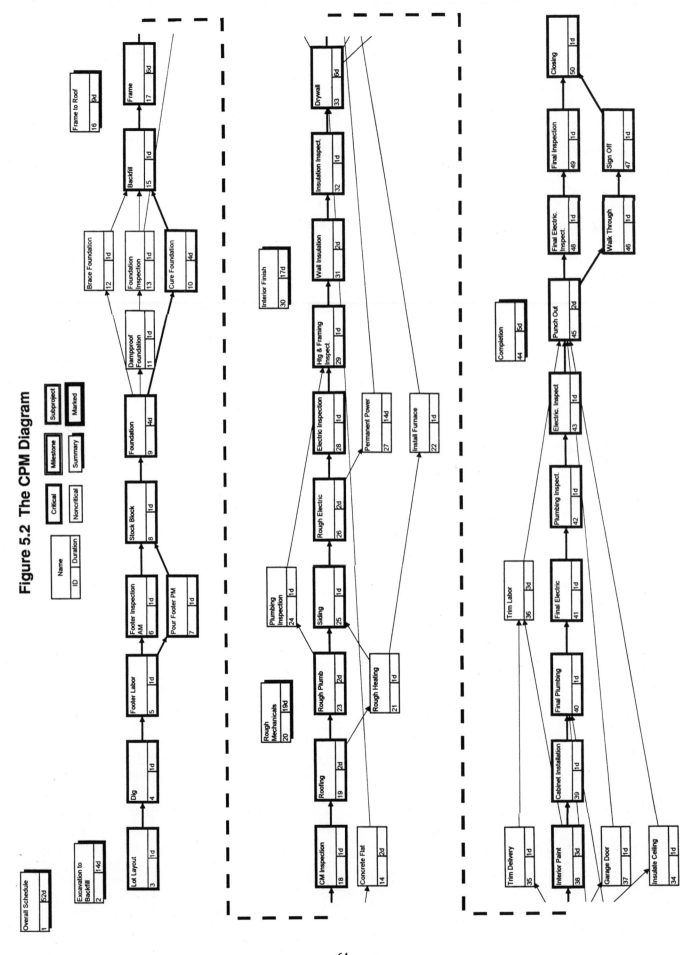

64

whatever the case may be. The computer automatically updates the schedule and makes adjustments to it as necessary. You can get an updated printout any time you wish. Material deliveries can be scheduled and will become easier to control. Finally, subcontractors can be lined up and schedule adjustments made more easily and accurately.

Scheduling Subcontractors

The only accurate way to schedule subcontractors is first to consult with each subcontractor and then negotiate a mutually agreeable duration for each activity. Resistance most often occurs when subcontractors are not offered an opportunity to participate in the scheduling process. Such participation should substantially improve subcontractors' willingness to establish realistic timetables and stick to them.

Several key points relate to a subcontractor's schedule:

- Hold a preconstruction scheduling meeting with all key staff, subcontractors, and suppliers involved on each major project, on complex custom homes, and periodically on production homes. This meeting encourages coordination and cooperation between subcontractors and suppliers and eliminates bottlenecks.
- Avoid scheduling two conflicting subcontractors on the same job, in the same place, at the same time.
- Have a job ready for the subcontractor on schedule; notify the sub immediately of any unavoidable delays.
- Send written notices to subcontractors reminding them when they are scheduled for a particular job.
- Encourage cooperation among subcontractors. If they suggest good, practical ideas on how to reduce cost or time and maintain quality, accept them.
- Base payment on compliance with the schedule. Subcontractors adhering to the schedule should be paid on time; if they delay the schedule, delay their checks to correspond exactly with number of days they delayed the job. Subcontractors soon get the message

when schedules are tied to checks. Interest may be imposed or penalty payments assessed if this stipulation has not been included in the contract.
- Reward superior performance. If the subcontractor is responsible for a substantial savings as a result of superior performance, reward that performance with a bonus and a letter of commendation.
- Negotiate with subcontractors who are not accustomed to working under a tight schedule. By negotiating from a position of knowledge and authority, you may find substantial time savings.

Chapter 6

Construction Team Building and Subcontractor Management

Introduction

Not so many years ago, a construction company's reputation was often based on the skill of the craftspeople on its payroll. In those days, skilled workers were a tremendous asset, and construction companies often did a large majority of their work with their hourly employees. The trend in residential construction in recent years has shifted toward subcontracting more and more of the job, with most companies subcontracting all of the work.

Hired Labor or Subcontractor?

Many factors enter into the decision to use hired labor forces or subcontractors for a particular construction job. You should weigh the advantages and disadvantages carefully before reaching a decision.

Advantages of Using Subcontractors

Whether their motivation is higher quality or lower capital investment, a majority of residential builders agree that the advantages to using subcontractors are many.

Greater Flexibility. The demand for new homes fluctuates greatly, particularly in relation to current mortgage interest rates. In times of high demand, building companies like to build as many homes as possible; when demand is low, they must be able to adapt to lower volumes of production. The more a building company relies on subcontractors, the easier it will be to achieve this increased or decreased output.

Less Risk. By subcontracting work, building companies transfer some of the financial, employment, and management risks to the subcontractor. Subcontractors are responsible for their own work. The builder has ultimate responsibility, but only when the sub refuses to honor his or her contractual commitments.

Less Capital Investment. Subcontractors often furnish material, labor, tools, and specialized equipment. In these cases, the building company can reduce its capital investment by avoiding investing in costly equipment that may sit idle much of the time, by paying subcontractors only upon completion of their work or only at regular intervals, and by lowering overhead costs.

Less Bookkeeping. Because the builder requires fewer employees and purchases fewer materials, less bookkeeping and less tracking of individual employee records are required.

Less Waste. When subcontractors supply their own materials, damage and waste tend to be kept to a minimum.

Less Overhead. By using subcontractors, builders do not need to purchase, rent, or maintain nearly as much equipment. In addition, with fewer employees, tax and insurance costs are reduced.

Improved Quality. Subcontractors usually specialize in one or two particular trades and become skillful and efficient in them. Therefore, the quality of work is easier to control. If builders establish acceptable quality standards before work starts, they can usually ensure this quality by withholding payment until the agreed-upon standards are met.

Scheduling. Because subcontractors are independent, a builder can stipulate in the contract that certain schedules be followed and that penalties will be imposed for noncompliance. One Chicago builder has used a "progressive network," a system requiring each subcontractor to notify the next one when his or her job is complete and the next step can begin. For this type of system to work successfully, you need good working relationships with all your subcontractors. Additionally, the notification requirement must be included in the subcontractor agreement.

Less-Detailed Supervision. Superintendents are usually not required to supervise the details of subcontractors' day-to-day activities, since subcontractors are responsible for their own work.

Disadvantages of Using Subcontractors

While the convenience of subcontracting work is an important factor to consider, using subcontractors is not entirely without drawbacks.

More Coordination. The superintendent spends more time coordinating work when using subcontractors. Each subcontractor is an independent business. It may be difficult for a superintendent to ensure that all subs perform their work in a timely manner according to the schedule and to the expected quality standards. Making last-minute schedule changes can also prove difficult.

Unqualified Subcontractors. Because of the low capital investment usually required, starting a subcontracting business is fairly easy. Many states require neither a license nor experience, resulting in a pool of subcontractors who may not be qualified to handle a job in terms of knowledge, experience, or adequate financing. This is an important concern, given that the ultimate responsibility for quality rests with the builder.

Supply and Demand. In good economic times when demand for housing is high, a sufficient supply of subcontractors may not be available. The few subcontractors willing to take on more work may be overextended and unable to meet all of their commitments.

Experienced Supervision Required. While less-detailed supervision is needed for experienced subs, superintendents must be qualified to distinguish high-quality work from substandard work. They must be prepared to recognize problems immediately, suggest alternatives, and converse intelligently with those involved in the trades.

Subcontractor Management

Finding qualified subcontractors can be a real challenge. There is a lot more to being a subcontractor than simply buying a pickup truck and a few tools. Hiring the wrong subcontractors can be devastating to the builder, while establishing strong relationships with good subcontractors can be key to a builder's success.

Qualities of a Good Subcontractor

It is important to know what to look for when you are trying to find the right subcontractor. Good subcontractors have a number of things in common:

- financial stability
- quality workmanship
- cost-consciousness
- ability to stay on schedule
- dependability
- cooperation
- adequate, competent work force
- prompt payment of their bills
- prompt service on call-backs
- ability to conduct business in a professional manner
- minimum material waste
- adequate insurance coverage
- adequate employee supervision
- fair prices

The Subcontractor-Superintendent Relationship

A cooperative relationship between subcontractor and superintendent is a vital aspect of a successful construction business. The relationship you have with your subcontractors can be the greatest determining factor in your success and the successful construction of your homes. Subs can literally make or break you. You should therefore encourage subcontractors to be active participants not only in the construction of your homes, but in the whole construction process. They should be encouraged to suggest new, more efficient methods, products, materials, or techniques.

While a subcontractor works for the building company in a relationship similar to that of an employee, the subcontractor is *not* the builder's employee. The relationship is best established by means of a written contract. Because the builder is the general contractor, with ultimate responsibility for the job, the builder should stipulate the terms of any contract with a sub.

Always keep in mind that a subcontractor must make a fair profit in order to stay in business. Builders and their superintendents should be careful not to take advantage of subcontractors who are inexperienced or who have made an obvious mistake in their estimating. These subcontractors may get the job for a cheap price, but you can probably count on work that is just as cheap. Disqualifying ridiculously low bids, or even giving a subcontractor the opportunity to back out gracefully, is usually better.

Locating Subcontractors

The best subcontractors are usually the busiest ones. To find good ones, you might contact your local home builders association, other builders, and other superintendents to find out which subcontractors they prefer. Suppliers and other subcontractors can also be excellent sources of names of new subs. They generally know how much business the sub is doing. In addition, they know how financially stable the sub is and will likely not recommend subcontractors who have a tough time paying their bills. Inspectors can also be excellent sources of information on subcontractor competence, since they see every subcontractor's work and are often in the best position to compare subs fairly to one another.

You can get a pretty good idea of how a subcontractor performs by inspecting other projects.

Consider the following questions as you examine the site:

- Is the job clean?
- Is the quality good?
- Does the sub work well with other people?
- Does the job sit for long periods without much progress?
- Are sufficient workers on the job to get it done in a reasonable amount of time, or does the job appear to move too slowly?
- Do workers have a professional appearance?
- How does the builder like working with the sub?
- How do the workers treat visitors?

Finally, check each potential subcontractor's current financial status with material suppliers (be sure to check with more than one) and credit bureaus.

Managing Subcontractors

As the superintendent, you must have the managerial ability to schedule, coordinate, and control all subcontractors on your job(s) so that work proceeds on schedule, within the established budget, and according to the quality specified. In addition, you will need to evaluate the managerial abilities of each subcontractor and determine if the subcontractor will be able to meet payrolls and overhead costs, pay suppliers, and still make a profit. Building companies in even the best financial condition may find themselves in difficult circumstances if subcontractors go broke in the middle of a job. Because the building industry is so dynamic and volatile, many builders have been seriously hurt by irresponsible or inexperienced subcontractors.

The Superintendent's Role

Your managerial role as a superintendent changes when subcontractors are used. Instead of being responsible for motivating and coordinating your own crew, you must direct and control highly independent subcontractors who in turn direct their own crews. You should therefore try to foster cooperation among subcontractors, particularly when their needs conflict, and mediate an acceptable resolution when necessary.

You can make the supervisory task smoother by ensuring that jobs are ready when a subcontractor arrives. Check the job out in advance. Subcontractors are often called in too early. Sometimes the superintendent assumes the job is ready when in fact the preceding sub is still not finished or the jobsite is not cleaned up. The result is costly extra trips. Make sure the preceding sub has finished and is out of the way. Subcontractors should be given as much lead time as possible to facilitate their scheduling and avoid last-minute decision making. In addition, every superintendent should inspect subcontractors' work in a timely manner so that any necessary changes can be made with minimal delay and expense.

Written Contracts

A wise man once said, "An oral contract is not worth the paper it's written on," and it is true that oral agreements can be difficult to enforce when disagreements occur. Yet many builders and superintendents continue to operate on a promise and a handshake for the following reasons:

- unfamiliarity with contract provisions and law
- reluctance of subcontractors to be bound by written agreements
- lack of standard contract procedures in many building companies
- ability of most subcontractors to perform adequately without a contract

Written contracts spell out a subcontractor's exact requirements and thus eliminate many areas of potential disagreement. The following provisions should be included in every subcontract agreement:

- plans and specifications
- quality of work
- scheduling requirements
- change order routines
- warranties and customer service
- penalties for failure to meet contractual provisions
- payment provisions
- cleanup policies
- other policies and procedures

- other general conditions, such as use of facilities, inspection requirements, and so forth
- liability, workers' compensation, and other insurance requirements, as applicable.

Plans and Specifications. Specifications must define as clearly as possible exactly what is intended in easily understandable terms of the trade. Occasionally, residential construction plans are superficial documents that don't begin to cover all of the important details. Poor specifications lacking a clear definition of how the house is to be built will confuse and frustrate subcontractors as well as homeowners. If superintendents and builders are not familiar with the options and alternatives available, they should consult specialists to establish the detailed specifications that will meet their needs and eliminate guesswork. Any additions or changes to the plans and specifications should be properly authorized and submitted with accompanying change orders.

Quality of Work. The quality of work should be identified in detail. With all of the different quality standards in construction, it is impossible for any subcontractor to know what you expect. Different builders do things differently. If you specify what you want in writing, your chances of getting it increase tremendously. Stipulate what you expect up front when you are interviewing and hiring the sub. Many builders have written standards of performance for each trade. These standards normally become a part of the terms of the contract.

Scheduling

Scheduling subcontractors is normally the superintendent's responsibility (see Chapter 5, Schedule Control). To expedite construction, a work schedule must be coordinated with each subcontractor. This schedule often becomes part of the contract to ensure the subcontractor's commitment. Progress meetings can also help in coordinating the smooth flow of construction operations.

A superintendent's positive action, particularly at the early scheduling stage, can prevent many complaints. Matters likely to create controversy should be decided as far in advance as possible, with the resulting decisions communicated to all parties. The superintendent can then spend less time arguing and more time seeing that work gets done.

Change Orders

Change orders tend to be a source of frequent disagreement if they are handled improperly. Keeping accurate records on every requested change is extremely important. Every change request should be documented through a formal change order procedure, including the following:

- request for change order
- change order cost estimate
- schedule update
- written approval signed by both parties
- change order deposit or payment
- completion of the requested change

The cost of the change order, as well as any increased costs related to rescheduling, should be passed on to the party requesting the change.

Warranties and Customer Service

Customer service is one of the primary sources of homeowner complaints against builders. Most buyers are satisfied with the homes on settlement day but become disappointed later when something goes wrong or they attempt to correct a mistake after move-in. The superintendent's frustration is compounded when he or she is unable to motivate the appropriate subcontractor to handle customer service calls in a timely manner. You can eliminate a great deal of confusion, delay, and frustration by stipulating subcontractors' customer service and warranty requirements in their contracts, including the time limits permitted. More detailed information on working with the buyer is included in Chapter 7, Working with the Buyer.

Payment Provisions

To the subcontractor, the most important part of the subcontracting process is payday. Provisions for payment should be clearly spelled out. Will the sub be paid weekly, in phases according to a percentage of completion, or only after the work is totally complete? What constitutes completion of the work? Who inspects the work to make sure it has been properly performed?

Policies and Procedures

Policies establish the philosophy of how the company will conduct business. Procedures, on the other hand, stipulate the exact manner in which business will be conducted. Establishing policies and procedures for both running a business and completing a job is one of the first steps a building company must take to prevent problems, avoid disagreements, and eliminate confusion. Policies and procedures for a building company might include the following:

- scope of work to be performed
- lines of authority and channels of communication
- acceptance of materials on the job
- proper conduct on the job
- use of site facilities
- acceptable and unacceptable construction methods
- use of equipment, materials, and temporary utilities
- provision of adequate crews on the job
- compliance with schedules
- safety and accident procedures
- protection of other subcontractors' work
- acceptance of the work
- payment policies and procedures
- lien protection requirements
- liability and other insurance coverage
- cleanup procedures
- call-back and warranty procedures
- special exceptions

These standard policies and procedures need not be written into every contract. They can be outlined as a separate document and simply referred to and included in the subcontract provisions along with the plans and specifications. Policies and procedures should be stated in a positive manner and should not be merely a collection of "don'ts."

The Dangers of Familiarity Versus Single-Source Suppliers

Although building companies often find it easier to deal with the same subcontractors on numerous jobs, the builder and superintendent must determine the relative importance of price, service, quality, and management complexity as they relate to subcontracting. One of the tenets of the Total Quality Management philosophy is the concept of a single-source supplier. There are a number of advantages to this concept:

- ease of estimating (because firm prices are regularly obtainable)
- ease and efficiency of training
- consistency of quality standards
- ease of working with familiar subs

However, using the same subcontractor on every job may cost more if the sub is not competitive. Building companies should avoid taking on additional costs merely to simplify subcontractor management.

If a building company does decide to use the same subcontractors on several jobs, superintendents must continue to check regularly to ensure that all subcontractors are remaining competitive and maintaining the builder's standards of quality. When a superintendent, builder, and subcontractors become too friendly, there is the danger that each side may begin to take the other for granted, leading to problems. To counter these problems, some building companies request competitive bids on each job as a matter of course. This practice ensures a more competitive price, provides better control, and maintains a higher level of service. In addition, you may want to check your subcontractors' financial status occasionally to prevent problems as a result of changing economic conditions.

Hired Personnel

When a building company chooses to perform the majority of its field work with its own hired personnel, rather than employ subcontractors, the superintendent's job changes markedly. You will be less concerned with coordinating various crafts and more concerned with planning work so that workers are kept busy for maximum productivity. The two superintendent functions essential to the success of personnel control are hiring and training.

The Nine Steps to Hiring Personnel

The following nine steps are crucial to effective hiring of construction personnel:

- Assess organizational needs.
- Prepare job descriptions.
- Assess current employees.
- Solicit potential candidates inside and outside the organization.
- Evaluate application forms and resumes.
- Conduct the initial screening and interviews.
- Check references.
- Conduct final interviews.
- Make a final selection.

Assess Organizational Needs. Most builders and superintendents face hiring problems when they fail to define their needs clearly at the outset. Prior planning is therefore essential to effective hiring.

Many superintendents fall into the trap of looking at their *wants*, rather than their *needs*. These superintendents usually end up hiring persons similar to themselves, believing that persons like themselves are most likely to be successful. While having a protégé can certainly satisfy a superintendent's ego, hiring workers with substantially different, yet complementary, backgrounds should offer greater rewards in the long run. With so many different and diverse skills required in the construction industry, it only makes sense to hire someone who will add to the building organization rather than fit an existing mold. For example, if existing personnel can estimate jobs but lack the ability to organize and schedule work, such attributes should be sought in new employees. On the other hand, if a building company has workers for framing and layout who are not as productive as they could be, you should look for a productive worker with qualities that will motivate others.

In assessing company needs, you will also want to do the following:

- Seek the opinion of those within the company who will be working with the new employee(s).
- Talk to subcontractors about any needs they see.
- Look at the competition. What type of workers make up their organizations?
- Talk to others who know the building industry in general, and your company in particular.

Prepare Job Descriptions. Once your company's needs have been clearly defined, job descriptions should be formulated to serve as checklists in assessing applicant qualifications and comparing them with the needs of the organization. These job descriptions should contain the following:

- all functions to be performed
- job responsibilities
- minimum qualifications and requirements
- description of resources available
- description of the extent of authority
- description of relationships with other members of the organization
- description of means of evaluating performance

Job descriptions may already be available for many positions. However, if company needs require a new or revised position, a new job description should be prepared. When preparing job descriptions, however, keep in mind that written job requirements should be objective and measurable. While personal attributes are more difficult to measure and evaluate objectively than technical skills, you should note attributes and abilities that the job requires, such as:

- knowledge of construction and practical experience
- initiative to get the job done and take necessary action
- ability to confront problems and deal with unpleasant situations
- oral and written communication skills
- leadership skills
- organizational skills
- listening skills
- ability to understand procedures and monitor processes and subordinates
- ability to manage stress
- ability to maintain consistent performance levels
- interpersonal sensitivity
- ability to learn and apply new information
- necessary mathematical skills
- an understanding of space relationships, particularly in visualizing shapes from drawings.
- mechanical reasoning skills

- reading skills to comprehend written materials with speed and accuracy

A complete and accurate job description is one of the superintendent's best hiring guides and can be particularly helpful when evaluating individuals for promotions and pay increases.

Assess Current Employees. Experts in personnel management constantly stress the importance of promoting an organization's present employees whenever possible. This preference over outside recruiting is understandable given the riskiness of hiring new people. Promoting current employees minimizes this risk, since the odds of objectively evaluating their skills, abilities, and knowledge is greatly enhanced. In addition, an environment that offers employees the opportunity to grow within an organization provides a healthy incentive to improve performance and tends to reduce turnover. Many large organizations have a policy that at least three people should be in training for each manager's job at all times. This policy gives continuity to the company and reduces the tendency toward crisis management.

Current employees should be evaluated according to the following criteria:

- Is the employee technically competent to do the job?
- Does the employee understand the complexity of the business and the role the job has in the company's profitable operation?
- Does the employee have a good record of attendance?
- Does the employee look for ways to become more productive—and make other employees and the job more productive?
- Does the employee get along with others? Can the employee motivate others to maximum performance?
- Does the employee have the potential to continue growing with the company, or is the employee below his or her maximum level of competence?

The extent to which current employees meet these criteria will determine how much recruiting will be necessary. If all requirements are met, you may not need new prospects. However, if current employees fail to meet the criteria, you may want to recruit enough outside individuals to conduct a comparison of all available candidates. If current employees simply are not qualified, more extensive recruitment will be necessary. Current employees who apply for jobs and are subsequently turned down should be informed of the reasons for their deficiency and the improvements required. If this task is done with tact and in a positive manner, it can motivate employees to greater performance.

While promoting individual workers within the building company can prove beneficial, new employees will inevitably need to be hired from outside on occasion. Hire new employees who have potential for growth. Planning for future needs is just as critical as planning for current needs. Too often, builders will wait until a crisis is imminent before giving much thought to hiring new employees; consequently, the company hires the first available reasonably qualified person, ignoring the long-term impact of this hurried decision.

Solicit Potential Candidates from Inside and Outside the Organization.
Recruiting potential employees is a skill that most managers need to develop and improve. A plywood sign at the construction site entrance is neither sufficient nor desirable. Rather than be interrupted constantly by drive-by applicants who may or may not have the qualifications needed for the job, the smart superintendent develops an awareness of where the good prospects are and how to reach them. For example, as a superintendent, you have contacts in the industry who can help identify qualified candidates. Other sources of potential employees include the following:

- everyday contacts on the jobsite
- subcontractors
- your file of potential candidates who applied for jobs earlier when no suitable position was available
- trade associations such as the NAHB
- educational institutes and schools
- material suppliers
- union offices
- building inspectors
- public employment offices
- private employment agencies
- advertisements
- competitors

Evaluate Application Forms and Resumes.
Job applications are useful tools for assessing an applicant's qualifications. They contain information on the individual's experience and background, as well as data required for record-keeping purposes. Application forms used by your company should include a release that the candidate must sign, authorizing you to make reference checks and verifying that all information on the form is accurate.

While resumes are rarely used in the construction industry, they should be requested of all applicants applying for management positions or other positions of significant responsibility within the organization. A resume can provide you with a concise statement of the applicant's education, work history, and other related experience. The resume also helps to demonstrate the applicant's communication skills.

Conduct the Initial Screening and Interviews.
Once all the necessary information has been gathered, you should review the information carefully and conduct the initial screening, weeding out candidates who are obviously unqualified or overqualified. This screening should result in a list of potentially qualified candidates to be interviewed.

While effective interviewing is the key to successful hiring, it is a skill few people master. You will find it well worth your time to develop interviewing techniques. These techniques will help you to assess each candidate's qualities and qualifications and provide each candidate with information about the job. While assessing candidates will be your primary concern, the latter responsibility should not be neglected. You want to provide sufficient information to allow the candidate to make a reasoned decision about joining your organization. In the initial interview, you would do well to focus on evaluating the qualifications of the candidate while giving only basic or sketchy information about the position. Generally, discussions about compensation and benefits should be reserved for the follow-up interview.

Prepare for every interview and set the stage for it. Before your first interview, determine what information is needed from applicants. Develop a list of questions you will ask all candidates. Based on the job application for each candidate, prepare additional questions appropriate for each individual candidate. As an effective interviewer, you should also review each candidate's work history to determine any unclear points and to avoid asking candidates to restate information already covered in an application or resume.

To achieve good results, candidates must be made to feel at ease. A casual atmosphere will help. You should not try to place the candidate in an inferior position by sitting behind a desk, but rather place two chairs facing each other in an informal setting. Make certain that you are not interrupted during an interview. In addition, good interviewers always try to follow the following guidelines:

- Allow sufficient time for the interview.
- Be systematic and organized.
- Rate all candidates on the same job-related criteria.
- Stick to the schedule.
- Allow time between interviews to evaluate candidates and prepare for the next interview.
- Do not oversell the organization or the job.
- Ask open-ended or probing questions that require more than yes or no answers.
- Avoid leading questions such as, "You like hard work, don't you?"
- Be fair. Do not discriminate.
- Give candidates all the information required to make a decision.
- Be personable, friendly, and considerate.

Keep in mind that all questions during the job interview should be job related. Avoid questions that may lead an applicant to reveal personal information. While this information may seem harmless and useful to have, the company may be open to legal action if a candidate alleges that another candidate was selected because of such personal information.

Check References. References should be requested of all job candidates. While references can sometimes be biased, they can be a good indication of where to look for additional, more objective information. If an applicant is a recent high school, trade school, or college student, you may find a transcript of credits helpful. You may even be tempted to do a little digging to uncover previous jobs that a candidate has not listed on an application or resume; contacting these employers or clients may provide much useful information. However, it may save time—and be advisable—simply to ask the candidate why this information was omitted. The candidate's signature on the application authorizes you, the potential employer, to contact the references *listed*. If later you find out references were omitted, you might simply disqualify the applicant on the grounds that the application is incomplete.

Checking candidate references will allow you to better judge each candidate's personal characteristics. Put your effort into assessing the candidate's compatibility with former coworkers, employers, teachers, and others. A history of jumping from job to job should be checked carefully to determine the real reasons for the moves. Thorough reference checking should reasonably determine if a candidate has a problem getting along with people or following through on commitments.

Conduct Final Interviews. Final interviews with top candidates will be necessary. Many builders and superintendents prefer to conduct these informal interviews outside the office, taking the candidate to jobs currently in progress. The ride time can be used to explain company goals and describe the position in detail. Problems pertinent to the new employee's work are explained. You may even ask the candidate to react to these problems and offer suggestions for possible solutions.

At some point during the final interview, you should provide each candidate with a detailed job description explaining exactly what the duties are and anticipated interaction with other employees. You may also want to introduce candidates to those with whom they will be working directly, if possible. If you will not be the future employee's immediate supervisor, that supervisor should thoroughly examine all top candidates as well and be given the responsibility and authority to make the final decision.

Make a Final Selection. At this stage, you should be familiar with the top candidates' attributes, abilities, and qualifications and be prepared to make a final decision. As emphasized at the start of this section, this decision to hire should be based on the company's needs and an applicant's ability to meet these needs.

Once you have made your decision, make an offer. Occasionally, superintendents and builders who have done a good job in the selection process make a tragic mistake at the last minute that may cause the entire process to fail: They try to get the person they want as cheaply as possible. They believe—usually mistakenly—that by keeping the price low, they can always bargain and raise the price later. Unfortunately, this practice can do a great deal more harm than good. Instead of the employee coming to work with a positive attitude and feeling good about the company, the employee may become suspicious and work below potential. Essentially, the old adage "You get what you pay for" holds true in this case. High-quality personnel are the single biggest investment a building company can make. The more invested in personnel, the more returned.

Fringe benefits, such as sick leave, vacation, insurance, and use of company vehicles can be just as important as salary. Several studies have attempted to determine the relative importance of various means of compensation. Almost without exception, salary was not at the top of the list in any of these studies, but fourth or fifth after proper recognition, opportunity for growth, good working atmosphere, and opportunity to use skills and knowledge.

Training Hired Personnel

Once hired, the new employee must be trained. Since the superintendent is responsible for training the field staff in new, more effective methods of construction, training and education are important keys to your success. They can make the difference between a growing, dynamic building company and a stagnating, declining one.

Training employees has several important advantages:

• Training improves job performance.

• Employees take pride in a company that devotes the time and money necessary to train its employees.
• Training is a two-way process. The "I care" attitude created often improves communication, which in turn encourages suggestions from employees that may improve performance.
• Training in safety procedures and methods reduces hazards and improves a company's safety record.
• The superintendent can train employees in the best and most economical ways to perform certain jobs, giving the company a competitive advantage.

Induction. Induction is the first important step in training a new employee. Effective induction procedures for each new employee can establish a positive attitude toward the new work environment for some time to come. During this initial period, the worker either confirms or changes his or her expectations of the building company.

Most jobs in a building company can be done many different ways, several of which are correct. New employees often are apprehensive about the way they have been taught and will probably take several days to adjust to changes in their new work environment. One means of easing this initially awkward period is to assign a particularly personable employee to work closely with the new employee for a few days to answer questions and help the new person adjust.

Orientation. Orientation is the next step, a time when the new employee becomes comfortable with the work environment. New employees are commonly concerned with the following during the orientation period:

• relationships with others in the organization
• tools and equipment policies
• payroll and timecard policies
• quantity and quality standards
• rules and regulations for conduct on the job
• involvement in apprenticeship programs (if applicable)
• advancement

Most of these concerns can and should be handled in a company policies and procedures manual. Unfortunately, many smaller building companies—and even some larger ones—have not developed these manuals. Superintendents and builders should create a company manual that helps each new employee answer six basic questions:

- What is my present position?
- What are my responsibilities?
- What are my rights?
- What limitations do I have?
- Where can I go from here?
- Where do I go when I have a problem?

Training Methods. Several methods are available to improve new and current employees' knowledge, skills, and attitude:

Apprenticeship programs, lasting from one to five years, are the traditional means of training tradespersons. By rotating from one operation to another and receiving related technical instruction, apprentices acquire additional skills, master the application of skills already learned with speed and accuracy, and develop independent judgment. This training method enables new workers to be productive throughout the training period. Studies have shown that workers completing an apprenticeship are more highly trained, work more steadily, learn new jobs faster, and are more likely to become supervisors than workers trained in other ways.

On-the-job training programs have proven successful for many building companies. Similar to traditional apprenticeship programs in many respects, on-the-job training rotates employees from job to job, giving them a broad background in various aspects of the building business. Experienced workers often are used to teach employees the necessary on-the-job skills.

Planned work activities can be an effective training method for specialized jobs. For example, carpenters and supervisors from an experienced crew can be asked to train workers in the more effective techniques used in wood-frame construction. This type of training can eliminate much of the expensive trial-and-error learning too common in the building industry.

Individual instruction may be necessary on occasion, to teach a worker a particular task. The training steps offered in Figure 6.1 may prove helpful.

Figure 6.1 How to Instruct

- Prepare the trainee.
- Put the trainee at ease.
  - a. Introduce yourself to the trainee.
  - b. Get acquainted.
  - c. Show the trainee the whole job.
- Eliminate fears.
  - a. Assure the trainee that he or she can learn the job.
  - b. Stress the importance of following and completing every instruction.
- Focus attention.
- Find out what the trainee already knows about the job.
- Select the one idea that offers the best starting point.
- Maintain the trainee's interest in the job.
- Explain what the trainee will gain (skill, knowledge, etc.).
- Spell out any ground rules.
- Explain the need to ask questions.
- Describe the format of the training.
- Present the key points of the lesson.
- Demonstrate and explain.
- Have the trainee do the job.
- Ask questions and encourage the trainee to ask questions.
- Review procedures and routines.

Chapter 7

Working with the Buyer

Introduction

As a construction superintendent, you will spend the majority of your time on the jobsite supervising the construction process. However, the fact remains that you also play an important role in customer satisfaction, in helping buyers achieve the "American Dream" of homeownership. Therefore, it is essential that you understand home buyers and their needs in order to meet those needs effectively and profitably.

Understanding Home Buyers

While this idea may seem a little odd to some, most new home buyers consider their homes an outward extension of all their hopes and dreams. Anything short of their mental picture of the perfect home can be devastating. The buyer probably came to the custom home builder or breezed into the sales office loaded with ideas fueled by magazines. These publications were likely full of glossy photo spreads of million-dollar homes and articles telling home buyers how to deal with builders and get the most for their money. While some of the buyer's ideas may have merit and others may not, the buyer may refuse to listen to reason or discuss a point rationally. Recognizing that a new home is usually the largest single purchase most people ever make may help you to understand what might otherwise be viewed as strange or erratic behavior on the part of the buyer. Try to look at the situation through the eyes of the buyer to understand motives and avoid potential problems.

One of America's most successful home builders has a favorite saying in the company:

There are three rules to customer satisfaction.

- The customer is always right.
- When in doubt, refer to rule number one.
- Even when the customer is wrong, he or she is still the customer.

This philosophy has worked well for the company over time. While building more than 500 homes a year, the company has a referral rate over 50 percent. More than half of the company's sales each year are a direct result of referrals from previous satisfied customers. Over 90 percent of its customers surveyed indicated that they would recommend the company to their family or a close friend. The company works hard to make sure that it builds a home that meets or exceeds homeowners' expectations.

Customer Relations

Your main goal as a superintendent is to maximize the company's profit while maintaining a high standard of quality. Earlier chapters have discussed how bringing the job in on time, within the budget, and according to the quality required is essential to achieving this goal. While accomplishing these three objectives is a key element in satisfying the homeowner, there is more to it than that. A superintendent who does all of the above yet fails to deal effectively with home buyers is not maximizing profits in the long term.

Why? Because the greatest asset a construction company can have is a good reputation. Happy, satisfied buyers will spread the word, and the two largest factors in buyer satisfaction are the quality of the work and *the way they were treated*. A third, related factor that can affect all areas of buyer satisfaction is time. You may often observe that the buyers of a house that falls behind schedule are more difficult to please in terms of quality and workmanship. Likewise, if the house is ahead of schedule, buyers may be more willing to overlook minor deficiencies. Keep in mind that many buyers feel that they are buying not only a new home but also a large dose of personal attention. Regardless of the size of your company and the number of houses you have under construction at any one time, homeowners are concerned with only one home—theirs. They expect the construction of their home to go without a hitch. If you can manage the construction of other homes at the same time, so much the better, but their home comes first.

The Superintendent's Role in Customer Relations

The role of a superintendent and the amount of direct contact with the client varies greatly from one company to another. In many larger companies, the superintendent has little interaction with the buyer. The customer comes to a sales office and selects a home and lot by discussing options with a salesperson. The superintendent builds the home from a set of standard plans and the customer moves in with little direct interaction with the superintendent. Customers may visit the jobsite from time to time while the home is under construction or they may not see it at all until it is complete. For such companies, it may be undesirable and confusing for the customer to be in direct contact with the superintendent.

Most small-volume and custom home builders conduct their business in a totally different manner. Often, the builder is working from plans provided by the homeowner or prepared by an architect. The homeowner—the customer—is an integral part of the construction process. Such customers are making decisions and selecting products for the home throughout the construction process. They visit the jobsite often and are heavily involved in making decisions. The superintendent and customer may meet together daily during crucial periods.

The builder and superintendent should set policies concerning the amount and type of interaction between the buyer and the superintendent. The lines of communication should be well established and well maintained.

Post-Sale Letdown

Every superintendent should keep in mind that a certain degree of "post-sale letdown," or buyer's remorse, is common after any purchase as large as a new home. Buyers suffering from this letdown usually have the feeling that perhaps they made a bad deal or have committed themselves to too much money. While it may seem like a job for the sales staff, you must do your part as a superintendent to reduce the stress. You can help by reassuring buyers of the wisdom of their decision. Simple statements such as "You're going to love living in this house," "This is a beautiful home," or "This is a great neighborhood," often help buyers conclude that their decision was a good one after all.

Policies and Procedures

Customer relations policies and procedures largely depend upon the contractual relationship existing between builder and buyer. For example, a job performed under a lump-sum or fixed-price contract puts you in more of an "arm's-length" relationship with the buyer than a cost-plus contracted job. With the latter, the buyer deserves to know not only the cost of different items of work but also *why* certain materials or procedures are being used. Another primary factor to consider is whether or not an architect is involved and to what degree. If an architect is involved, he or she can be enlisted to help answer a buyer's questions and explain construction procedures.

Custom builders should carefully spell out policies and procedures regarding lines of communication, frequency of visits to the jobsite, and other situations involving interaction with the customer. Many builders make it a standard policy that the superintendent communicate with the homeowners weekly to keep them informed on the progress of their home.

Increasing Buyer Understanding

Builders should insist that all buyers understand exactly what they are buying. A key reason to hold the preconstruction conference with the buyer is that it presents the opportunity to set the customers' expectations (see Chapter 2).

For example, most buyers find it hard to visualize the actual home on the basis of construction drawings. By showing a model with comparable room sizes, layouts, and details, you can enhance the buyer's conception of the true finished product. Providing this attention within reasonable limits can be the key to smooth relations with buyers. Perhaps even more is consistent understanding of the expected quality of finishes. If the buyer was shown a model or other sample home, you must ensure that the buyer's home meets or exceeds the model in every respect.

Some buyers, unfortunately, will remain unsatisfied even when the home meets or exceeds the quality of the model. For example, Buyer X had sold his first home and was moving up to his dream home. He had seen examples of the builder's finished product and seemed satisfied with its quality. One night, after his house was completed, Buyer X held a spotlight up against the walls and marked each and every imperfection. In addition, he complained that the tops of the door casing in one of the closets had only one coat of paint. While the builder agreed to try to fix the drywall imperfections, he explained to Buyer X that these flaws would not be noticeable under ordinary lighting conditions. To prove the point, the builder took Buyer X and his spotlight back to the home Buyer X had lived in for years and showed him large imperfections that had earlier gone unnoticed. In addition, an inspection of the tops of the door casings in the old closets revealed not only the absence of a second coat of paint, but the absence of any paint at all.

Obviously, handling extreme cases like this one with tact and understanding can prove difficult at best, but the dividends can be great. You must always remember that you are a professional and you should conduct your superintendent duties in a professional manner at all times. By doing so, you can often turn a potentially bad situation into one that enhances your company's long-term reputation.

The Importance of Contracts. When dealing with home buyers, whether in relation to a custom home, semi-custom home, or completely speculative home, there is no substitute for a good contract that touches all the bases and is easy to understand. Buyers naturally fear "snake oil deals" and contracts with the proverbial "small print." A good builder or superintendent will take time to make certain the buyer understands everything in an agreement. One of the purposes of the preconstruction conference is to review the contract requirements in detail. It has been the experience of many builders that you have to remind buyers constantly of their obligations under the contract especially when building custom and semi-custom homes. Buyers tend to forget what is required of them and the time frame in which things must be decided and completed. Many builders find it helpful to list homeowner responsibilities as activities on the project schedule and give homeowners weekly reminders of responsibilities.

Buyer-Requested Changes. An important area to discuss with every buyer (and include in every contract) is the policy regarding changes to the work. If an architect is involved, his or her understanding of change orders should smooth the process considerably. In any event, two things must be made clear regarding changes:

- One pre-designated person will authorize changes on behalf of the company.
- All changes will be written and will include an exact description of the change, the difference in the sales price, and the change in schedule, if any.

This policy is especially important to follow on cost-plus homes and in custom home building. In a Maryland court case, a builder failed to keep the buyer up to date on cost overruns on a cost-plus job*. The builder subsequently had to absorb these overruns because he failed to keep up with them in an orderly fashion and keep the buyer informed. The court ruled that cost-plus jobs are different from ordinary fixed-price contracts in that the builder owes the buyer a duty to act in the buyer's best interests. Therefore, the

* *Jones v. H. Hiser Construction Company, Inc., 484 A.2d 302.*

builder was obliged to keep up with the overruns so that the buyer could make appropriate adjustments as required.

The role of the superintendent should be carefully defined by the builder with regard to change orders. Does the superintendent have the authority to approve change orders? Can the superintendent price out change orders? How do you mark up change orders for overhead and profit? What does the superintendent do in case of emergency? At a bare minimum, the superintendent should be kept completely up to date on the status of all change orders. See Figure 7.1 for an example of a change order form.

Buyer Visits and Company Contacts. Some construction companies have policies stipulating when buyers may visit the jobsite. Some companies also pair each buyer with a contact person within the company to answer any questions that may arise. With most buyers, such procedures are unnecessary. However, a buyer will occasionally come along who is on the jobsite constantly, asking questions of everyone. Such buyers are usually just showing a keen interest and curiosity and do not realize that their presence is disruptive to the normal job rhythm. The issue of who owns the lot that the home is being built on is also a factor in your buyer visit policy. In certain cases, you will have to make buyers aware—in a tactful manner—that the builder is not trying to hide anything or get away with shoddy workmanship or substandard materials. Explain that, in order for the job to flow smoothly, jobsite visits must be at preappointed times and questions must be channeled through one person. This contact person may be the superintendent or someone on the sales staff.

Good communication is probably the most important key to happy homeowners. In most cases, home buyers will be much more comfortable if you maintain good communication with them. People require different levels of communication. Some want to be left entirely out of the picture. "Call me when it's done," is their philosophy. Others want to be deeply involved. They may require a daily phone call and frequent site visits. Determining a mutually acceptable level of homeowner involvement and communication is important. Even once estab-

lished, the level of communication may change from time to time. For example, when the house is being framed or in the finishing stages, the homeowner may need more communication than when the footings or drywall are being done. At critical stages it may be wise to increase the frequency of communication. One thing is sure; being proactive in communicating with the homeowner is much better than addressing customer complaints.

Conflict Resolution

Conflicts arise among the various parties on construction projects practically every day. As the superintendent—particularly if you are also the builder—you will arbitrate many of these disputes. For example, if one subcontractor has damaged the work of another, it is your responsibility to ensure that the parties resolve the problem fairly.

Disputes with buyers are somewhat different in that the superintendent has a greater vested interest in the outcome. You will find that establishing and following procedures, particularly the types of procedures discussed in this book, are the easiest ways to avoid or settle these disputes.

Handling Buyer Conflicts

When you find yourself involved in a conflict with a home buyer, remain calm and act in a professional manner. If you remain calm, this will help the buyer also remain calm. The skill of listening is essential. Learn to listen with an empathetic ear so as to understand the position of the buyer. First, find out what the buyer's concerns are. Make sure that you understand the real problem. Sometimes people may address symptoms rather than problems. For example, one home buyer expressed extreme concern over the progress of construction on his home. He was deeply upset by even minor delays. When the superintendent got to the bottom of the issue, however, he found out that the homeowner had absolutely no savings and was concerned about being out of his apartment on an exact date in order to save the last month's rent and be able to pay the closing costs on the mortgage.

Figure 7.1 Change Order Form

Buyer: _____   Lot number: _____

Contract dated: _____   Plan: _____

Item number	Description of change	Cost	Schedule adjustment
_____	_____	_____	_____
_____	_____	_____	_____
_____	_____	_____	_____
_____	_____	_____	_____
_____	_____	_____	_____
_____	_____	_____	_____
_____	_____	_____	_____
_____	_____	_____	_____
_____	_____	_____	_____
_____	_____	_____	_____
_____	_____	_____	_____

Totals: $_____ _____ Days

The changes listed above, and the corresponding costs and adjustments in the construction schedule, have been requested by you, the purchaser. By signing this change request, you agree to pay for indicated changes and acknowledge that the construction schedule and estimated delivery date for the referenced home are revised accordingly. Change requests will be incorporated into the home only after they have been approved and signed by the builder.

Approved: _____   Purchaser: _____
Builder: _____   Purchaser: _____
Date: _____   Date: _____

Source: Carol Smith and William Young, *Customer Service for Home Builders*, (Washington, DC: Home Builder Press, National Association of Home Builders, 1990).

Once the superintendent understood the real problem, finding the solution was relatively simple.

Once you understand the position of the buyer, then make sure what the position of the company is before you offer a solution. State your position in clear and simple terms, giving all the reasons or justifications for your position. If the issue pertains to specific contract language or to policies that have been conveyed previously to the homeowner, reiterate them in a tactful, nonconfrontational manner. You must then evaluate both positions in a fair-minded way. If you determine that the buyer is right, admit it and take appropriate action. However, you must remember that a fine line exists between exercising the golden rule and giving away the store. Admissions of responsibility or liability made by a superintendent in a spirit of appeasement can used later in the courtroom to win an otherwise weak case.

If the buyer's position is weak or based on faulty reasoning, you should tactfully point out the fallacies in his or her argument. Take care to use thoughtful words in these instances in an effort to smooth an already sensitive situation.

Cramming something down a buyer's throat may give the superintendent some momentary emotional satisfaction, but this action carries a high price in decreased goodwill and reputation.

Often, through some quick but creative thinking, you can come up with a win-win solution, one where both the owner and the builder come out ahead. In the situation mentioned above, where the owner was concerned about closing costs, the superintendent was able to offer to do some additional work on the home which the homeowner had anticipated doing in exchange for a slight extension of time on the project schedule. Although the homeowner presumably had to work out his rent and closing costs dilemma on his own, the additional finishing work on the home was worth the extra time. The superintendent got additional time to complete the project, the homeowner got some extra finishes on the home, and both came out ahead.

Daily Job Log. Many superintendents keep a daily job log or diary. Conflicts and resolutions should be entered religiously, since notes made when something happens carry a great deal more weight than notes made afterward in the unhappy event that you end up in court. While no one wants to end up in court, it takes only once to make you realize the importance of proper documentation, however time-consuming it may seem. In order to make the daily job log more convenient, consider carrying a small tape recorder with you with a tape for each job. As the project progresses, you can record pertinent information on the tape. A recorded log may not carry as much legal validity as a written record, but it is not a bad substitute and it is relatively painless.

After Completion

Another critical time in a customer relations program occurs just after the construction is complete. The superintendent will be required to handle any punch list items, and service the home with warranty callbacks in an organized fashion that enhances—rather than diminishes—customer goodwill. The customer's demands will not always coincide with builder policy. However, effective, common-sense procedures, combined with tact, good listening skills, and a

willingness to please, can go a long way toward eliminating much of the disagreement common in post sale customer service work. One of the keys to good customer relations is a written warranty. It need not be complex or increase the obligations of the builder. In many areas, builders are required by law to warrant a home for one year. It is better to have both parties sign a written warranty agreement spelling out what is covered under the warranty than to face continual disagreements about what is covered and what is not.

Scheduling Customer Service Calls. Random, spur-of-the-moment customer service calls waste time and money. If you are given the responsibility of handling customer service calls, you should schedule them according to a regular, manageable time table. This scheduling procedure should be in writing and should be made clear to all buyers—either by sales and customer service staff or by the superintendent.

This type of scheduled customer service is usually based on one or more scheduled after-sale service calls: one at 30 to 60 days after closing and often another just prior to one year. Buyers are asked to keep a record of minor problems for correction at these regular intervals. Many companies increase buyer goodwill by conducting these callbacks even when there are no obvious repairs to perform, dropping by simply to answer questions and explain any unclear operating procedures. Of course, emergency service should be provided immediately on an as-needed basis.

Often, other service work is required. In many small companies, superintendents are responsible for coordinating this work. They must determine the nature of the problem and decide on the proper remedy and who would be best to perform the work. Sometimes the superintendent will make the corrections him- or herself, but most of the time it will be necessary and proper to have a qualified subcontractor make the corrections. This makes subcontractors aware of the quality of work the customer expects. Timely completion of customer service work is essential to the success of the company. Keep close track of customer service requests and how long they take to complete.

Figure 7.2 Work Order Log

Contractor: _____   Phone: _____

Date		Work order no.	Name of homeowner	Comment/Completion log
Issued	Expires			

Source: Carol Smith, *Warranty Service for Builders and Remodelers*, (Washington, DC: Home Builder Press, National Association of Home Builders, 1991).

Subcontractors and Customer Service. If your company is small, you will probably depend on subcontractors for much of your service work. Good communication and effective record-keeping are your best way to ensure timely, quality customer service work from subs. Do not shift a customer's complaint to a subcontractor just to get rid of it, but do direct service calls to the subcontractor responsible for the problem whenever possible. Your company may wish to consider using standardized four-part forms to write up work orders for subcontractor callbacks. You should keep one copy and give the remaining copies to the sub; upon work completion, one copy remains with the sub, one copy with the customer, and one copy is sent back to you (or the customer service office, if applicable). If additional compensation is warranted, the last copy can contain a request for payment. Figure 7.2 shows an example of a work order log.

Keep in mind that prompt attention to service requests is a key component of good customer service. Remember, the customer doesn't care *who* is responsible for the mistake or does the work, only that it get done—properly and quickly. You may therefore wish to form an agreement with your subs that asks them to as-sign certain days or hours of days to perform callback work. Some builders require that subs contact customers within two days of receiving a customer service request to schedule a service appointment. They may also require that the work be completed within a reasonable amount of time (within two weeks).

Warranty Service Voucher System. Many large-volume and production builders offer their customers a special voucher system that provides for callback service while providing an incentive for customers to perform their own small repairs rather than request service callbacks. Such a system begins with an account opened in the name of the buyer for a predetermined amount, such as $200. Special vouchers are then given to the buyer, each worth $20, for use in requesting callback service. Service work is then paid for with the vouchers, and any funds remaining in the account at the end of the warranty period are returned to the buyer, with interest. These programs have proven extremely successful and may prove effective in your company if carefully managed.

A Final Word

Residential building is one of today's most exciting and challenging businesses, and one in which the construction superintendent plays a large and important role. The feeling that comes from successfully organizing people, materials, and equipment to create a beautiful and functional home can be quite special. When you pass a home that you helped to build years earlier, you probably find it difficult not to look at it with at least a small sense of pride and think, "I built that!"

This pride is at the heart of true success in the construction business. The truly successful are often not those who are wealthy or brilliant, but those who are genuinely good at what they do and take pleasure in it. In turn, most people who are good at what they do apply simple rules and goals to their tasks. This book has attempted to present such simple rules, targeted at maintaining your budget, complying with your schedule, and establishing quality control, leading to maximum profits—and an irreplaceable feeling of total success—in the long term.

Increase Your Business Knowledge with These Bestsellers

Contracts and Liability for Builders and Remodelers

Contains valuable contract language that can be inserted directly into your own model contracts. ISBN 0-86718-376-4. $25

Customer Service for Home Builders

Provides proven techniques for operating an effective, yet inexpensive, customer service program regardless of your company's size. ISBN 0-86718-355-1. $15

Estimating for Home Builders

Contains all you need to know to produce complete accurate cost estimates, including information on computerized estimating. ISBN 0-86718-372-1. $28

How to Hire and Supervise Subcontractors

Learn how to work more efficiently with subcontractors. ISBN 0-86718-366-7. $15

Production Checklist for Builders and Superintendents

Use this comprehensive checklist to complete projects on time and within budget. ISBN 0-86718-351-9. $20 book only, $35 with diskette, $25 diskette only.

Scheduling Residential Construction for Builders and Remodelers

Explains current techniques for scheduling residential construction projects, both manually and by computer. ISBN 0-86718-401-9. $29.

Software Directory for Home Builders and Remodelers

An annually updated directory of software packages programmed just for home builders. Organized into 11 different categories listing hundreds of software packages. Quick-reference grid lets you compare programs at a glance. ISBN 0-86718-399-3. $15.

Your Business Plan: How to Create It, How to Use It

Let this guide take you through the creation of a strategic business plan. Includes a model business plan based on an actual small-volume building company. ISBN 0-86718-390-X. $22

To order any of these books, or request an up-to-date catalog of Home Builder Press titles, write or call:

Home Builder Bookstore®
1201 15th Street, NW
Washington, DC 20005-2800
800-223-2665

NAHB MEMBERS RECEIVE A 20% DISCOUNT ON ALL BOOKS

Prices are subject to change.